STUDYING FICTION

Studying Fiction provides a clear rationale alongside ideas and methods for teaching literature in schools from a cognitive linguistic perspective. Written by experienced linguists, teachers and researchers, it offers an overview of recent studies on reading and the mind, providing a detailed guide to concepts such as attention, knowledge, empathy, immersion, authorial intention, characterisation and social justice.

The book synthesises research from cognitive linguistics in an applied way so that teachers and those researching English in education can consider ways to approach literary reading in the classroom. Each chapter:

- draws on the latest research in cognitive stylistics and cognitive poetics;
- discusses a range of ideas related to the whole experience of conceptualising teaching fiction in the classroom and enacting it through practice;
- provides activities and reflection exercises for the practitioner;
- encourages engagement with important issues such as social justice, emotion and curriculum design.

Together with detailed suggestions for further reading and a guide to available resources, this is an essential guide for all secondary English teachers as well as those teaching and researching in primary and undergraduate phases.

Jessica Mason is Senior Lecturer in English Language at Sheffield Hallam University, UK. She has published widely in the fields of cognitive linguistics, stylistics and English education.

Marcello Giovanelli is Senior Lecturer in English Language and Literature at Aston University, UK. He is the author of ten books and over thirty research articles and book chapters in literary and applied linguistics, and in English education.

'This book made me think more clearly about how the students in my class encounter literary texts and articulated the important distinction between giving my students authentic reading experiences and teaching them about a particular book. The book poses some difficult and interesting questions about the way we present literature to our students and the very particular practice of classroom reading. The book is especially useful in helping to unpick and make sense of the complexity of reading in the classroom and helping the reader to do the same within their own context. Whilst there are numerous texts on how to teach reading in primary schools, as a secondary teacher I found this refreshing and thought provoking as well as useful in offering ways of reflecting on my teaching myself and with my department.'

Myfanwy Edwards, Curriculum Leader for English,
Richmond Upon Thames School, UK

'In what can only be described as a highly sophisticated exploration of the reader experience, Mason and Giovanelli guide the reader through the extraordinary journey of our interaction with fiction. *Studying Fiction* sets about tackling the complexities of text engagement: from authorial intent, through to the moment we decide to take a book in our hands for the very first time, both writers scrutinise the process in which we make meaning from texts, and how in turn, they nourish our future selves. Far more than a framework for reading within the classroom, *Studying Fiction* puts forward contemplations around how we form relationships with fiction: from the deliberations at play during the decision to read a book, to the emotional undertaking as we grieve for our fictional favourites, *Studying Fiction* enables the reader to understand what it means to read, providing teachers with the necessary comprehension to teach reading as a thing of beauty, beyond the constraint of an examination paper. An essential read for any teacher who wants to actualise just how powerful reading fiction can be.'

Kat Howard, Assistant Principal,
The Duston School, Northampton, UK

'In this book Mason and Giovanelli offer a cogent and engaging discussion of what it means to study, teach and read fiction. Drawing on their own research and expertise, as well as pertinent research in the field, they skilfully align theory with practice, making this book a usable read and reference for university students, academics, and teachers alike. One of the most appealing parts of this book is how the authors' passion for English and education emanates from each chapter and is then channelled into a series of useful reflections and activities in each chapter section, bolstered with key takeaway points throughout. This book is a rare find that bridges theory and practice in an accessibly academic way, even going as far as to rationalise and provide a solution to the bane of every English teacher's life: "This makes the reader want to read on."'

Ben West, Achievement Lead and Teacher of English,
The Garibaldi School, Mansfield, UK

STUDYING FICTION

A Guide for Teachers and Researchers

Jessica Mason and Marcello Giovanelli

Routledge
Taylor & Francis Group

LONDON AND NEW YORK

First published 2021
by Routledge
2 Park Square, Milton Park, Abingdon, Oxon OX14 4RN

and by Routledge
52 Vanderbilt Avenue, New York, NY 10017

Routledge is an imprint of the Taylor & Francis Group, an informa business

© 2021 Jessica Mason and Marcello Giovanelli

The right of Jessica Mason and Marcello Giovanelli to be identified as authors of this work has been asserted by them in accordance with sections 77 and 78 of the Copyright, Designs and Patents Act 1988.

All rights reserved. No part of this book may be reprinted or reproduced or utilised in any form or by any electronic, mechanical, or other means, now known or hereafter invented, including photocopying and recording, or in any information storage or retrieval system, without permission in writing from the publishers.

Trademark notice: Product or corporate names may be trademarks or registered trademarks, and are used only for identification and explanation without intent to infringe.

British Library Cataloguing-in-Publication Data
A catalogue record for this book is available from the British Library

Library of Congress Cataloging-in-Publication Data
Names: Mason, Jessica, author. | Giovanelli, Marcello, author.
Title: Studying fiction : a guide for teachers and researchers / Jessica Mason, Marcello Giovanelli.
Description: Abingdon, Oxon ; New York, NY : Routledge, 2021. | Includes bibliographical references and index. |
Identifiers: LCCN 2020051420 | ISBN 9780367150648 (hardback) | ISBN 9780367150662 (paperback) | ISBN 9780429054792 (ebook)
Subjects: LCSH: English fiction--Study and teaching (Secondary)--Great Britain. | English language--Style--Study and teaching (Secondary)--Great Britain. | Cognitive grammar.
Classification: LCC PR824.5 .M27 2021 | DDC 823.0071/2--dc23
LC record available at https://lccn.loc.gov/2020051420

ISBN: 978-0-367-15064-8 (hbk)
ISBN: 978-0-367-15066-2 (pbk)
ISBN: 978-0-429-05479-2 (ebk)

Typeset in Bembo
by SPi Global, India

For Ron Carter

CONTENTS

List of figures   x
List of tables   xi
Acknowledgements   xii

1 Introduction   1
    1.1   Focus of the book   1
    1.2   Cognitive linguistics   2
    1.3   Cognitive poetics   3
    1.4   Structure of the book   3
            Further reading   5

2 Why study fiction?   6
    2.1   Why study fiction?   6
    2.2   Why promote reading?   10
    2.3   Studying fiction in schools   11
    2.4   The Cox models   13
    2.5   English in the universities   14
    2.6   'Cambridge English' and 'London English'   15
    2.7   Concerns about equity   16
            Further reading   19

3 Identity   20
    3.1   Reading in context   21
    3.2   Studying fiction as a type of reading experience   22
    3.3   Booktalk and power   24
    3.4   *Talking About Texts: Reading and Identity* Project – an overview   26
    3.5   'As a teacher': reading and professional identity   30
    3.6   Lying about reading, and what it means for English   33
            Further reading   34

4	Text choices		35
	4.1 Decisions, decisions		35
	4.2 Practical parameters		36
	4.3 Schema theory		38
	4.4 Narrative schemas		40
	4.5 Text choice and equitable education		44
	4.6 Paracanons		46
	Further reading		47
5	Attention		48
	5.1 Understanding attention		48
	5.2 Attention and reading		49
	5.3 Attention and text analysis		51
	5.4 Thematic figure-ground		51
	5.5 Burying		52
	5.6 Burying and reading		53
	5.7 Attention in the classroom		56
	Further reading		63
6	Readers		64
	6.1 Reading as response		64
	6.2 Reader-response theories and education		65
	6.3 Louise Rosenblatt's transactional theory		67
	6.4 Text World Theory		69
	6.5 Disbelief, relevance and criticality		78
	Further reading		79
7	Writers		81
	7.1 The writer and meaning		81
	7.2 Models of the writer		83
	7.3 Working with models of the writer		89
	Further reading		96
8	Emotion		97
	8.1 Why do we read?		97
	8.2 Feelings		100
	8.3 Modelling characters		101
	8.4 Characters, enactors and selves		105
	8.5 Empathy and social justice		107
	Further reading		109

Coda	110
References	112
Appendix: *Talking About Texts* survey	120
Index	124

FIGURES

3.1	Responses to Q7: Would you call yourself 'a reader'?	28
3.2	Books read per year reported by respondents to the *Talking About Texts* survey	29
3.3	Concordance snapshot for the phrase 'as an English teacher', sorted alphabetically by words to the right	31
5.1	Figure and ground	49
6.1	Text-world of *The Small Hand*	71
6.2	Remote text-worlds in *The Small Hand*	73
7.1	Fictional entities	84
7.2	Screenshot from Heider and Simmel (1944)	85
7.3	Shakespeare classroom display	91
7.4	Multiple authors classroom display	92
8.1	How reading changes behaviour (from Alsup 2015: 71)	108

TABLES

2.1	A comparison of 'knowledge deficit' and 'critical pedagogy' views	17
3.1	Professions of *Talking About Texts* participants	29

ACKNOWLEDGEMENTS

We would like to thank Kat Howard, Megan Mansworth, Gwen Nelson and Holly Wimbush who read early versions of some of the chapters of this book and provided many useful suggestions for improvement. Ben West reviewed a full draft of the manuscript for us and we are grateful for his substantial insights and comments, which have undoubtedly improved our final version. We are grateful to Megan Goodes and Rosie Georgiou for allowing us to reproduce images of their classroom displays in Chapter 7.

We would also like to thank the students we have taught on our respective English education modules at Aston University, Sheffield Hallam University, University of Nottingham and University of Sheffield. Students and teachers wanting to find out more about stylistics and cognitive poetics should look at the programmes on offer in the English departments at these institutions. We have also had the pleasure of discussing reading and studying fiction with numerous teachers at the various workshops and conferences we have attended and run over the last five years. We are grateful to everyone we have taught and worked with; all of you have helped to shape the ideas in this book.

As always, we are grateful as ever to our colleagues, families and friends and would also like to acknowledge the support of the team at Routledge at the various stages of writing.

Finally, Jessica Mason would like to extend special thanks to Ben Hannam and Kate Longson, without whom her involvement in the final preparations of the manuscript of this book would simply not have been possible.

We are grateful for permission to reproduce parts of the following research papers in Chapter 2 of this book:

"Well I don't feel that": *Schemas, worlds and authentic reading in the classroom*, by Marcello Giovanelli and Jessica Mason, *English in Education*, 2015, reprinted by permission of the publisher (Taylor & Francis Group, http://www.tandfonline.com)

"What do you think?" Let me tell you: Discourse about texts and the literature classroom, by Jessica Mason and Marcello Giovanelli, *Changing English*, 2017, reprinted by permission of the publisher (Taylor & Francis Group, http://www.tandfonline.com)

1
INTRODUCTION

This chapter will:

- provide an overview of the book;
- discuss cognitive linguistics and cognitive poetics as key disciplines underpinning our coverage of topics;
- outline the content of the remaining chapters.

1.1 Focus of the book

This book is aimed at teachers and researchers interested in the teaching of literature and in examining the ways books get studied and talked about, both in and out of educational settings. Throughout the book, we draw on different kinds of research and analytical methods but largely draw on an approach to the study of fiction that has its roots in stylistics and cognitive linguistics.

Stylistics is 'simply defined as the (linguistic) study of style [which is] the way in which language is used' (Leech and Short 2007: 1). Stylisticians believe that all language, whether found in a literary work, from Shakespeare to Walliams, or in a newspaper, an advert, a tweet or even this book, is made up of conscious and unconscious choices about which various words, phrases and larger structures to use. Stylisticians argue that using our most recent knowledge of linguistics to unpick and understand these choices, and the styles that result from them, is the best way to approach any text, of any genre, mode or period.

In this book, we adopt the principles of stylistics both in some of the analyses of texts that we undertake, and in the way that we broaden out some of its parameters to explore studying fiction in education more generally. In this latter respect, we draw on recent developments across cognitive linguistics to inform a cognitive stylistic or *cognitive poetic* approach. In each of the chapters, we discuss key topics related to reading through a cognitive poetic lens, and suggest ways that the discipline offers insights that may be useful to the teacher in order to make decisions in terms of how they conceptualise, plan for, and deliver activities that involve reading fiction.

In the remainder of this chapter, we introduce some basic cognitive linguistic principles, and then provide an overview of cognitive poetics, a field which has focused on the role of the mind in literary reading but which we now extend out to examine reading in education contexts. Following this, we outline the structure of the book by summarising each of the focuses of the remaining chapters. The chapter ends, as with all the chapters in the book, with some recommendations for further reading.

1.2 Cognitive linguistics

Cognitive linguistics is an umbrella term for a broad discipline that covers a number of approaches concerned with the relationship between language and the mind. Broadly speaking, cognitive approaches to language emphasise that:

1. Our thought results from our interaction with the physical material world, including our sense of space and being around other people. The ways in which we conceptualise ideas and events are heavily influenced by this principle of *embodiment*, for example in how we use metaphors to explain abstract ideas through more familiar concrete ones.
2. We store knowledge in domains or *schemas* which are flexible and dynamic, and shift and develop as a result of our experience in the world. When we read, schemas are activated by words in the text which help us to understand the contents and interpret meanings. In other ways, the text itself may help to build up a schema, for example if we are reading something on a topic with which we are unfamiliar. So, our schema of London in the nineteenth century might be developed through reading some of Dickens' novels.
3. Language therefore provides a point of access to stores of knowledge that we have built up over time. When we come across a particular word, some aspects of the schema are always activated while other types of knowledge are only activated in more specific contexts. For example, 'train' activates general knowledge about a mode of transport, but when reading Dickens' *Dombey and Son*, 'train' might instead call up only very specific knowledge about trains in the Victorian period (or at least an understanding that trains in the nineteenth century were different to those now). We also use these schemas to help us imagine other states of being, future events or things that we simply want to happen. These ideas are central to the ways that we engage with books.
4. There are continuities between language and other cognitive processes: for example, we use the same arrangement strategies in language to foreground some things and background others as we do when we look at a scene. The choice of one grammatical form over another can therefore always be considered as motivated and meaningful – as a kind of packaging-up of events for a particular purpose.
5. Language is a social phenomenon and involves people guiding each other's attention. In the case of reading, the participants are author and reader, and in the classroom there are also teachers, and students. Interactions, and understanding them, are therefore really important.

Our approach in this book is an applied linguistic one in so far as we argue that teachers can use concepts and theories from linguistics as a way not of teaching content (although this may happen too) but rather as a theoretical backdrop to their own practice; what Carter discusses as the difference between 'teaching linguistics' and 'having linguistics as a foundation for classroom language teaching' (1982: 8).

Halliday (2002) conceptualises this important point in his distinction between 'grammar' and 'grammatics'. Whereas 'grammar' is the phenomenon studied, Halliday defines 'grammatics' as a pedagogical framework that teachers can use 'to think with' (2002: 416). Like Carter's 'foundation', Halliday's 'think with' highlights the ways that linguistic approaches can underpin ways of conceptualising learning and teaching in the classroom. In previous publications, we have argued for a 'cognitive grammatics' (Giovanelli 2014, 2016; Giovanelli and Mason 2015) as an applied cognitive linguistics for the teacher to use as a means of examining various aspects connected to studying fiction in education. This book represents an extended application of that idea, here specifically in the service of thinking about studying fiction in the classroom.

1.3 Cognitive poetics

In essence, whilst retaining all of the principles of stylistics, cognitive poetics additionally recognises the value that recent and ongoing discoveries in cognitive linguistics and science can offer. As Mason (2019: 13) explains:

> Where cognitive poetics takes its exploration of reading as interaction a step further [than stylistics] is in its recognition that narrative understanding and response necessarily involves a central concern with what happens in the mind as we engage with and reflect on stories. As such, it posits that research on cognition offers a wealth of knowledge which is highly salient to understanding the behaviours and experiences of real readers.

In this book, we extend the scope of cognitive poetics by demonstrating its value specifically within educational contexts related to the study of fiction. We import our 'cognitive grammatic' approach into the studying of fiction and matters of interpretation in and beyond the classroom. In doing so, we address questions such as:

- What happens in our minds when we read?
- How and why can readers get so engrossed in a book that they lose track of time and surroundings?
- How can two people read the same text and have very different responses and interpretations?
- What is the role of authors in the process of making meaning?
- Why and how can people feel sad when a fictional character dies?
- How can reading generate emotional responses such as grief, fear and empathy?
- How might teachers influence, through their text choices and classroom practices, the ways that young readers respond to texts?

In this book we explore the cognitive poetics of studying fiction.

1.4 Structure of the book

The subsequent chapters of this book are set out as follows.

In Chapter 2, we explore the history and practices of reading and literature teaching in schools, offering an overview of practice in English education and various shifts that have taken place, particularly in the last hundred years. In particular, Chapter 2 will reflect on what different emphases within the study of fiction have communicated to young people and practitioners about what studying fiction is 'for', and what it means to be a 'good reader'. It explores the origins of the oft-invoked false dichotomy of language or literary study within subject 'English', and maps its consequences for the two fields of study, both the intentional and the unintentional. We introduce the discipline of stylistics, which has acted as a bridge and a synthesis for these two apparently distinct branches of English, and offer some preliminary outlines of the value of this approach for the study of fiction. Though we discuss some of the history of English as a subject in England, the specifics of this evolution in this particular country is not our main focus. Rather, we simply use this version of the field's history to draw out questions and debates that have and continue to be asked the world over. These questions include: Why study fiction? Which fiction? How? With who? To what end? Answers to these questions are not categorical, and the history of this practice offers insight as to different configurations of the literature classroom.

In Chapter 3, we examine the school, and specifically the English classroom, as a space where reading takes place. We will think about reading in these more formal academic contexts relative to other settings where books are read, discussed and analysed, such as universities, book groups, in the course of socialising both face-to-face and online. It highlights that many reading practices in school classrooms, especially when studying set texts, are relatively unusual both in terms of what we ask readers to do, and when we ask them to do it. The second half will then explore the findings of the *Talking About Texts: Reading and Identity* project, an anonymous survey of over six hundred people, with over two thirds of participants working in some sort of education role. The questionnaire explored concepts such as honesty, embarrassment and judgement, and asked respondents to share their feelings about reading as well as their experiences of talking about books with other people. These findings are examined in terms of their implications for teachers and students engaged in identity-formation through studying and talking about fiction.

In Chapter 4, we examine discourses about children's and Young Adult literature and canonical texts, contemporary popular texts and 'the classics', in relation to the study of fiction. The chapter provides a precis and critique of the most common points of debate and conflict regarding text choice for academic study. It explores different perspectives on the value of different kinds of texts, including a pragmatic acknowledgement of many of the constraints practitioners typically operate within, and hopes to provide a clear set of the most salient considerations for educators and researchers reflecting on which texts merit academic study.

Chapter 5 examines the concept of attention from cognitive psychology and linguistics and recontextualises it in the literature classroom. Drawing on our own research we outline the principle of 'pre-figuring' and examine how classroom activities and the classroom space itself may divert students' attention to specific ideas and interpretations with both desirable and undesirable outcomes. For example, reflecting on common practices such as asking students to read a stretch of text each, and how this splits attention between becoming immersed in the story and monitoring their physical environment for their turn.

In Chapter 6, the focus turns to readers. In this chapter, we outline a number of ways in which the role of the reader has been theorised and provide an overview of Louise Rosenblatt's transactional theory: a model of reading that has had significant influence over the years. From there, we outline the cognitive discourse grammar Text World Theory which draws on a similar set of principles to transactional theory in that both argue meaning arises from readers acting on cues in the text and fleshing these out using various types of background knowledge. We argue that Text World Theory offers a useful way not only of conceptualising the reading process and analysing texts, but also offers a framework for the teacher to think about how tasks might be set up.

In Chapter 7, we address the thorny issue of intentionality and the role of the writer. Here we examine a number of ways in which authors have been viewed as more or less central to the reading experience and outline work by David Herman and Peter Stockwell who both propose that making inferences about writers' intentions is a central part of how we experience books. We argue that these debates have interesting implications for how we conceptualise and talk about books in classrooms, how we frame literature through classroom displays and how we devise assessment questions for students.

Chapter 8 focuses on emotions. Our approach here is to argue that emotional responses to reading fiction have as much place in the classroom as they do in private reading experiences. We explore a number of ideas related to the value of allowing responses to be driven by emotional connections to texts. We then move from readers' emotions to characters' emotions. Extending our discussion of Stockwell's notion of how we model the minds of authors when we read, we outline two cognitive approaches that explain how we position ourselves with characters when we read. Drawing on research which has focused on the pro-social benefits of reading fiction, we argue that attending to personal feelings and empathetic responses in the classroom offers an alternative pedagogy that allows for a radical re-evaluation of how fiction could be studied.

Finally, in Chapter 9, we summarise our thoughts and present what we believe are the most important insights that a cognitive poetic approach to studying fiction offers those interested in reading and teaching literature.

Throughout the book, we encourage you to consider how the ideas we present relate to your own practice. To this end, each chapter has a number of 'Activities and Reflections' questions which we have placed at strategic points. These questions are designed to encourage you to think about the chapter content, either on your own or in discussion with colleagues, and offer the opportunity for you to reflect on, and offer alternative ideas related to, the practice of teaching English. Some of these questions are straightforward, but we hope that many will involve taking more time, outside of this book, to consider the implications of the chapter contents for yourself, your department, your school and your students.

Further reading

Carter (1982) is still one of the best overviews of why linguistics can provide such an enabling set of principles for classroom practice. The concept of 'grammatics' is introduced and discussed in Halliday (2002). Good applications of 'grammatics' can be found in Macken-Horarik (2009, 2012), taking a functional linguistic angle, and Giovanelli (2014) from a cognitive linguistic perspective. Cognitive poetics is introduced and discussed with reference to recent advances in the field in Stockwell (2020). Our own paper (Giovanelli and Mason 2015) is a good introduction to some of the ideas we discuss here, and which are developed throughout this book.

2
WHY STUDY FICTION?

This chapter will:

- advocate for 'authentic' reading as a central focus of English;
- explore some of the history of English as a school subject and academic discipline;
- outline some of the key considerations that inform beliefs about the aims and purposes of studying fiction;
- explore some different ideological positions concerning the purposes of education in general and the study of fiction specifically.

2.1 Why study fiction?

In his discussion of the history and purpose of English teaching, Gibbons (2017: 1–2) writes that the subject has been characterised by a series of ongoing debates around its identity. As he argues:

> A schooling in English is powerful, or it is dangerous – or it is both, depending on one's own perspective. Sophisticated users of language in all its forms are able to question, to criticise, to challenge. Little wonder battles have been fought, won and lost over what English should look like for children.

Activities and Reflections

1. What are your instinctive responses to this quotation from Gibbons? How far do you agree or disagree?
2. In your view, what are the most powerful (or dangerous) potential purposes of English in general, and of the study of fiction specifically?

There are many potential reasons to study fiction. In England and many other countries, the most pressing reason in schools is because it is a staple of national tests (here called GCSEs and

A-levels). This is, as every teacher who has answered a room full of young people's questions about why they need to learn something with 'because it's on the exam' will be well aware, not a very persuasive justification.

One consequence of the fact that studying at least some works of fiction is, for many teachers and students, a 'must', is that there often isn't the space or motivation to reflect on why we do it, and what, in an ideal world, we would like studying fiction to achieve. We believe that careful consideration of this question is vital, because the ways in which we engage with fiction in schools, what we say, and the texts we study, both tacitly and explicitly shape the subject of English. Furthermore, these decisions are likely to have powerful and long-reaching influences on young people's sense of what reading is and whether they enjoy it. These beliefs will then go on to inform the attitudes towards reading of the adults those young people become. In a very real sense, therefore, society's engagement with reading is in no small part constructed in the English classroom. This book offers that space for reflection.

In this chapter we begin by exploring some of the visions of literary study that have been offered by various schools of thought at different points in history, and advocate specifically for the importance of young people having what we term 'authentic' reading experiences when they study fiction.

Activities and Reflections

1. In your view, what's the point of studying fiction?
2. How do you perceive the relationship between studying fiction and reading for pleasure? What in your experience is it? What in your view should it be?

2.1.1 The case for 'authentic' reading experiences

There is no 'typical' reading experience. We read in all manner of places, for all manner of reasons, and in all manner of ways. Neither are our reading experiences all the same; books are different, circumstances change and we are different readers from one text to the next (Stockwell 2013). Thirty students in the same class will all engage with and experience the same text differently, though there may be broadly similarities, because they all bring different knowledge, experiences, tastes and contexts to the text with them: all reading experiences are in some senses necessarily unique. However, in this book, we argue that there are certain features that can make a reading experience *authentic*, and we promote throughout the book what we term *authentic reading* in the English classroom. As outlined in the previous chapter, this book adopts a cognitive linguistic approach which closely complements existing work in the field of reader response theory (e.g. Rosenblatt 1938; Hall 2009). This defines reading as a transaction between text and reader (this is discussed more expansively in Chapter 6). In this sense, reading is always a subjective and necessarily personal experience; although the text remains static, readers inevitably differ in the range of resources they bring to the reading experience in the form of their own background knowledge, their past experiences, tastes, interests, preferences, and reading competence. This transaction can be understood as a two-stage process where initial experiences and impressions then evolve into something more critical and coherent. This process of revision is intuitively familiar to readers and was described by author Stephen King at a talk at Lowell University:

> Any good book, you should be able to read it twice. The first time, what I want from you is your total attention, and I want you to be engaged. I don't want you to be analysing, thinking about the language, um, I don't want you to see me at all. I don't want to be part of that equation. But if you come back to it again, I would like to think that there would be something else, as well.
>
> (King 2012).

This, we argue, describes the essence of an authentic reading experience. By 'authentic' we mean a reading that is born out of an individual's initial process of unmediated engagement with, and then incremental or reflective interpretation of, a text: doing the latter requires the former. This is what typically happens when a person reads a book they enjoy: they read the words on the page and build rich mental representations of the world of the text (see Chapter 6), sometimes becoming absorbed in that world and perhaps losing track of time (see Chapter 5). As they read they may pause and think about what they have read so far, try to guess what will happen next, form and change their attitudes towards different characters, empathise with or come to hate them, hope for plot points to happen or not, experience physical sensations such as slowed breathing or increased heart rate, laugh out loud, perhaps even cry, and so on. Upon finishing the book, they may make a final assessment of how good or bad they thought it was, reflect on different aspects, talk it over with others, mentally revisit sections and themes or even physically go back to earlier chapters to look again. Then they may move forwards in their lives with a unique mentally archived version of the story locked away in their memory (Mason 2019), now available for them to call up and draw on again in future, either privately or in the course of social interactions with others (discussed further in Chapter 4).

Stockwell (2002: 31) discusses this in terms of 'interpretation' and 'readings', with interpretation being the iterative and incremental interactions between reader and text described above, and a 'reading' being the end result of that process:

> interpretation [is] a holistic understanding of the literary work that begins [...] even before we begin to read the actual text. [... It] is what all readers do when encountering literature, when the experience is ongoing and as yet unexpressed. As soon as readers become aware of what they are doing, this more analytical stage of recognition can be differentiated as reading.

These two symbiotic practices form the essence of any considered, critical reading experience. However, assessment systems around the world and across stages place a strong emphasis solely on the latter – the 'reading' that forms the end product – not the engagement with the text and the stages of authentic 'interpretation' that came before it. This is because, simply, the end product is much easier to test. This is certainly no criticism of teachers, who are stuck within a system they are then tasked with navigating, but this unfortunate fact does create inherent risks to authentic reading in educational spaces. For a student to engage in authentic reading, they must have space to interpret the text, to experience it for themselves. In this book we explore, from a cognitive linguistic perspective, the ways by which English teachers might support students in turning their interpretations into rich, critical but also authentic readings.

If interpretation is imposed on a student, the resultant reading is likely not to be authentic, but instead *manufactured*. *Manufactured readings* are learnt, not made; they occur when readers are denied the space to engage in their own process of interpretation. Manufacturing is the practice of learning about a text, rather than engaging with it. It is perfectly possible to talk competently about a book drawing only on a manufactured reading; in fact Pierre Bayard (2008) wrote about this in his *How to Talk About Books You Haven't Read*. It is reasonable to suggest, therefore, that if a test assesses a student's ability to reproduce a reading, rather than undertake interpretation, they could parrot back a learnt, manufactured response they have accrued from discourse they have heard *about* the examined text, from their teacher, their peers, or things they have read or watched about it online, and still do well. In fact, closed book examinations actively encourage this kind of manufacturing to some degree because they require students to write about the text without direct reference to a copy of it. What they have not done, however, is anything that could be realistically described as reading or interpretation.

This is not to say, of course, that there is no space for learning about texts within the literature curriculum: knowledge about books, even if we haven't read them, can be a powerful thing. A weighted emphasis on 'literature as knowledge', however, conceives studying fiction more as literary history than developing skills of critical reading, response and analysis. Equally, we are not suggesting that it is unimportant for young people to garner knowledge about the texts they read. Indeed, authentic and manufactured reading should be properly thought of as a cline, not a binary, with an experience that is purely one or the other fairly unlikely. A fully authentic reading experience with no imposition of external interpretation prior to reading whatsoever would essentially require never having heard of the book before reading it. In reality, this is unlikely: readers encounter discourse about books prior to reading them all the time, often actively seeking this out in the forms, for example, of recommendations, reviews or even the blurb on the back. All of these may perform small degrees of manufacturing – influencing their thoughts and responses as they move forwards and read for themselves. Equally, an entirely manufactured reading would also be unusual as this would involve no direct interaction between the reader and the text at all. A more accurate and useful way of thinking about authentic and manufactured reading, therefore, is as a cline on which it is possible to comparatively situate different reading experiences. Different class reader unit designs, for example, can orient towards offering students more authentic or more manufactured experiences of reading depending on their emphasis. Units that foreground students' direct engagement with the text and give space for them to articulate, develop and reflect on their own thoughts, interpretations and responses, for example, will tend to offer more authentic reading experiences. By contrast, units that give primacy to teaching students about texts, learning quotations or received interpretations of others (from literary critic to teacher), especially if student response is downplayed, will typically orient towards producing more manufactured reading experiences.

Thus, whilst we are not suggesting that all courses focusing on studying fiction should seek to be fully authentic, we do argue that a key aim of literary study should be to provide students with ample opportunities to experience authentic reading wherever possible. We advocate this on four grounds. First, the research is clear that young people who read for enjoyment do better in every aspect of education, and are the most likely to achieve academic success. Reading experiences in school that resemble reading for enjoyment are therefore vital in nurturing and encouraging this. Second, for students who do not read for enjoyment, their understanding of what reading is, whether they like it, and whether they could see themselves as a reader will likely be shaped by their experiences of studying texts in school. Simply put, without authentic experiences, these young people are likely to make these assessments based on a highly skewed notion of reading. Research has shown that teachers and students are very much aware of the impact studying can have on 'reading for pleasure' (Nash 2007; Nightingale 2011). They describe this difference in a variety of ways, but it generally manifests in a sense of 'something getting lost' in the context of overpowering assessment and accountability regimes (Maybin 2013; Turvey and Lloyd 2014).

In the simplest possible definition, an emphasis on authentic reading in schools can be described as the opportunity to avoid, or at least mitigate, some of this 'loss'. Third, there is certainly value in students learning about texts, and gaining knowledge about literary works, but learning about texts is not reading. Reading involves an interaction between text, reader, and author: without a strong representation of authentic, direct engagement with texts in English we would argue there is a fundamental dissonance between the subject in theory and in practice. Fourth, manufactured readings are largely non-transferrable because they are necessarily text-specific. If literary study focuses too strongly on teachers educating students about fictional works then they risk keeping those students in a position of dependence, because they are learning responses, not having them. Authentic engagement, on the other hand, necessarily involves cultivating skills of personal response and analysis, which can ultimately empower students as independent critical readers of *any* text, not just the select few they have studied.

This conceptualisation of English coheres with the desires of the majority of practitioners, who believe that the study of literature should engage students deeply on a personal level, encouraging them to develop a strong sense of emotional investment in their reading (Goodwyn 2012). However, both historically and in the current climate, it has been argued that many assessment systems have stifled creativity and delegitimised certain kinds of student response and teaching practices (Dymoke 2002; Ofsted 2011). Equally, increased teacher accountability, performance-related pay, league tables, and the high-stakes nature of the profession can encourage a 'teach to the exam' mentality that teachers feel compelled to adopt (Au 2007). In these conditions, manufactured readings can fare just as well, if not better, than authentic ones since teachers have undoubtedly more control over what is perceived to be the correct way of responding to literature (Mason 2014). Although this type of practice has the potential to seem like a safer option to some teachers, depending of course on myriad factors including experience and confidence, the danger remains that students can end up being taught about books, rather than how to read them.

2.2 Why promote reading?

There are important questions that teachers and policy makers should consider about the processes and practices of reading per se. Cliff-Hodges' (2009, 2010) research focuses on young people who actively self-identify as 'readers': they reveal that they see reading as an imaginative leap, carrying them away to alternative and sometimes fantastical fictional worlds, and as a type of simulation on which their everyday concerns can be run. Her interviews also highlight the emotional investment that young people put into reading (see also Dungworth et al. 2004; Cremin 2010). In this way, reading becomes shaped and defined as the fundamental human drive to make sense of the world by drawing on connections between reading and one's own experiences, memories, and other texts that the individual has encountered (Cremin and Myhill 2012; McCallum 2012).

This personal and emotional investment places reading as intricately tied to both individual-personal and wider social group concerns, and highlights the array of schematic knowledge that young readers hold, draw on and use when reading. The importance of background knowledge and resources to students' educational success is well documented (Daw 1996; Clark and Rumbold 2006; Clark 2011). However, much top-down policy-making over the last twenty years has downplayed the influence and importance of personal and literary experiences and other domains of knowledge on students' responses to literature.

And yet the reasons for studying literature that are offered by young people provide an opportunity for teachers to consider how best, in designing classroom tasks, to use information about motivation, emotional investment and the kinds of background knowledge and resources that students bring with them. In doing so they can both encourage and facilitate the kinds of rich and meaningful reading practices that are often unnecessarily lost in the study context.

This raises an important question: if both teachers and students tend to be in favour of authentic reading in school, how and why does it get lost?

2.3 Studying fiction in schools

There are specific challenges for studying fiction as an aspect of the academic curriculum which has a direct correlate, reading for pleasure, out in the world. In particular, in the course of discussions about education it is often easy to generalise as though all subjects are the same, when in reality they can be extremely different. An excellent historical example of this in England, for example, was the idea that tasks in a lesson should not exceed twenty minutes, on the basis that children cannot reasonably be expected to pay attention to the same thing for longer than this period (outlined in the Key Stage 3 Strategy and the Framework for Teaching English in 2001). This may well have been the case for some tasks, but it was clearly wrong to suggest that this would be the case for all, given that tasks and subjects are not homogenous. In practice, this led to unnecessary transitions within a lesson, with activities only sometimes slightly differentiated from one another in an attempt to honour this principle. It is no wonder many teachers may be sceptical of research when ideas like this are distorted and generalised on such a scale. For English lessons, some schools and teachers may continue to heavily fragment reading of the actual text as a hangover of this practice, even when the text itself is the apparent focus of the unit. At the same time, many, many children read fictional works for hours at a time (English is in this regard privileged to have direct corollaries in the world outside school where we are able to see this is the case). Anyone with a young bookworm in the family will know that whichever activities this may be the case for, reading books certainly isn't one of them.

Another example of an historically popular generalised principle that took no account of subject-specificity in England was the notion that teachers must be able to show their students making progress in every lesson, which may still exist in some schools. Again, there may have been some merit to this idea in reference to other subjects, possibly even some aspects of the English curriculum, but in relation to the study of lengthy texts this has had problematic and profound implications. Namely, this idea eroded the status of reading the text, and made it difficult for teachers working in contexts employing this policy to simply read the work being studied for extended periods. Here, a strategy that is pedagogically sound and appropriate is delegitimised as a result of pronouncements that did not take subject-specificity into account. Furthermore, this risks degrading the perceived importance of engaging with the text itself.

These are just two examples that illustrate the profound importance of thinking carefully and critically about how more general suggestions and research about education apply both to a particular subject and even the different aspects of that subject's content.

Other reasons for the downplaying of the importance of authentic reading can be found in the historical tensions surrounding the purpose of English as an academic subject, which have existed in one form or another since its inception. The study of literary fiction has dominated both secondary curricula and examination specifications in England since the beginning of the twentieth century. Generally speaking, there have been two opposing positions about its purpose. The first, initially influenced by the Leavisite tradition of scholarship that revolutionised English teaching in both secondary and higher education (see Hilliard 2012), presented the study of literature as close reading and the extraction of meaning, promoting the authority of the text, and the production of literary-critical responses. In this classroom, the teacher's role is often to disseminate information and to validate understanding; the approach taken is one of direct instruction (Brooks and Brooks 1993). The second stance is more reader-centred, involving an epistemology of reading in classrooms that is rooted in understanding response and viewing interpretation as dynamic, complex and socially-oriented. Realistically, many teachers tend to take a combination of these approaches, with a sensible middle-ground consisting of degrees of teacher input together with opportunities for students to engage with their own ideas in discussion with others.

2.3.1 A broad church or a rag-bag?

The breadth of subject English, whilst attractive in many ways, is another significant challenge for the discipline. Once labelled by O'Malley (1947: 57) as a veritable 'rag-bag of all the subjects', it is little wonder that English has persisted as a site of argument and debate about its value and purposes (more so, we would argue, than any other school discipline). At varying times, afforded different degrees of space and importance, English has included: functional literacy – that is, teaching students to read and write; the punctuation, grammar and spelling of Standard English; oracy; the study of literature with a big or a small 'L' – which may include poetry, Shakespeare, other plays, novels and short stories; cultivating personal response; fostering imagination; creative writing; skills of critical analysis and interpretation; learning *about* texts; the study of language and linguistics; drama; media, and genre writing.

Activities and Reflections

1. Left entirely up to you, which of the topics above would form the focus of English as a subject, and why? What factors would inform your decisions?
2. Who do you think is best placed to make decisions about which aspects of the English curriculum should be prioritised for a particular class at a given time or stage? Why?
3. Do you think all of these areas discussed above really belong within English or would they be better placed elsewhere (or removed entirely)?

For English in particular, then, concerns about how to split the limited and valuable resource of time across the multitude of different areas the subject is tasked with covering are likely to be especially acute. In other words, the weight of these decisions is likely to bear even more heavily on English than on other departments. Equally, this is fertile ground to encourage impositions of hierarchical judgements about the relative importance of different areas: it can easily become a question of what deserves or merits time, and therefore also what does not. This risks putting different elements of the subject into competition with one another, with often not even heads of department able to make decisions about which are selected. In the context of school league tables, progression-based pay, and accountability culture, this hierarchy is often more likely to be informed by what is perceived of being of most value for students undertaking high-stakes assessments, rather than most valuable in a broader sense.

2.4 The Cox models

Debates surrounding the purpose of English have raged since the subject's inception, and historically were discussed in a long line of government reports, starting with the Newbolt Report in 1918 and ending with the Cox Report in 1989. The absence of reports of this kind since then are not an indication of resolution, but rather a consequence of the fact that the introduction of the National Curriculum in 1990 eclipsed the need for such reports. The disputes have subsequently been enacted in relation to the contents of the National Curriculum instead.

The 1989 Cox Report is particularly notable and of relevance to the current discussion because it compiled a holistic list of five possible views of English, each encompassing a different vision of the core aims and purpose of the subject. These are:

1. A '**PERSONAL GROWTH**' view focuses on the child: it emphasises the relationship between language and learning in the individual child, and the role of literature in developing children's imaginative and aesthetic lives.
2. A '**CROSS-CURRICULAR**' view focuses on the school: it emphasises that all teachers have a responsibility to help children with the language demands of different subjects on the school curriculum.
3. An '**ADULT NEEDS**' view focuses on communication outside the school: it emphasises the responsibility of English teachers to prepare children for the language demands of adult life, including the workplace, in a fast-changing world.
4. A '**CULTURAL HERITAGE**' view emphasises the responsibility of schools to lead children to an appreciation of those works of literature that have been widely regarded as amongst the finest in the language.
5. A '**CULTURAL ANALYSIS**' view emphasises the role of English in helping children towards a critical understanding of the world and cultural environment in which they live. Children should know about the processes by which meanings are conveyed, and about the ways in which print and other media carry values.

(DESWO 1989: 60).

It is important to note, however, that whilst these models are often invoked and discussed in isolation, and it is productive to discuss different possible aims of English in these terms, Cox envisaged that all five models would potentially be used at different points and stages: we are not supposed to have to choose one and eschew all the others! Nonetheless, this can be the way in which conversations about the relative value of different areas within English's 'broad church' unfold, and it is easy to note a particular division arising amongst some of these models between, for example, prioritising literature and prioritising language study.

Activities and Reflections

1. Which of the Cox models do you feel the most affinity with, and why? (You can choose more than one if you want to.)

In fact, as we will repeatedly return to throughout this book, there can be very different and equally legitimate purposes for studying different works in different ways. We would suggest that this is one way in which the tendency to retreat into apparently binary camps can be really unhelpful, because it de facto encourages the notion that there is a single definitive answer to why we should study fiction, or indeed to the purpose of education itself. Instead, we advocate for more nuanced reflections about the most valuable approaches to a particular text at a particular time, and discussion of how the delivery of a specific unit or course matches and supports intended aims.

2.5 English in the universities

Conflicting ideas about the focus of English as an academic discipline, as well as an uneasy marriage between language and literature, also arose around the subject when it was introduced in universities, as well as in schools. Interestingly, however, the hierarchy in higher education was positioned in reverse, with language viewed as the more serious and academic element of the subject, essentially there to bolster and prop up the credibility of literary study as a legitimate pursuit.

In universities the same union of language and literature took place from the inception of English as an academic subject around a similar time as schools: Oxford's School of English was established in 1894, with Cambridge following suit slightly later in 1919. Interestingly, however, this umbrellaing of both language and literature under the auspices of 'English', occurred for quite different reasons than the ones proffered in earlier phases of education. In the universities, language was used as the means by which to legitimise the study of fiction as a 'proper' intellectual pursuit. Cameron (2012: 15) explains:

> The project of establishing English as a reputable degree subject in British universities depended, among other things, on showing that it made intellectual demands which bore comparison with those of the traditional classical curriculum. Critics who disputed that were fond of remarking that a course of study could hardly be called rigorous if it allowed you to earn a degree by simply reading novels and poems in your own language. One way in which that objection was countered was by injecting into the English curriculum a substantial dose of philology: Old English, Middle English, and the history of the language. These areas of study demanded a kind of discipline which are thoroughly familiar to classicists; Anglo-Saxon might be less ancient than Greek and Latin, but it was certainly no less dead, and there was no shortage of grammatical paradigms to be mastered before students could turn their attention to poetry.

This framing of poetry as an easier aspect of the subject may well not be shared by many teachers and students today. In fact, there is a wealth of research showing that the study of poetry is typically viewed as one of the most challenging and anxiety-provoking elements of English for teachers and students alike (see, for example, Weaven and Clark 2013; Xerri 2013). This casting of literature as the fun and more frivolous partner of the rigorous and more testing language study similarly represents an inversion of the relative status of the two branches of the subject in many secondary schools today. It is also apparent that the study of language as it is conceived here is vastly different from the iteration in schools and indeed most universities today, with the study of Old and Middle English typically now packaged up within the remit of literature. Areas of linguistic study which had yet to emerge as substantive sub-disciplines such as sociolinguistics and discourse analysis are nowhere to be seen, but have now come to dominate language study in British schools and universities.

2.6 'Cambridge English' and 'London English'

Part of this shift in the emphasis of language study, and therefore English, arose much later, in the 1940s and 1950s, with the emergence of 'London English'. It is the case today, on paper at least, that we provide secondary education for all young people. This had not always been the case. Whilst education for all was an aspiration, and in spite of Arnold's explorations as early as the mid-1800s of how formal education could be tailored to the benefits of the so-called 'working class', free secondary education for all did not become a reality in England until the late-1940s (see Gibbons 2013 for a detailed and insightful exploration of this period of English education). Thus, although English was introduced in 1904, free school provision was not widely available and most children did not attend school past the age of 12. This was extended to age 14 by an act passed in 1918 which also tried to remove fees from schools. However, the economic depression of the 1920s quickly followed, and this meant much of the act was not implemented in practice. As such, 'academic' school subjects remained, in reality, the preserve of the privileged, and though grammar schools did offer free places to children from less advantaged backgrounds, these were few and far between.

The meaningful opening up of secondary education in the UK coincided relatively closely with the founding of the National Health Service (NHS) with the passing of the Butler Act, which expanded free secondary provision to all. As with the NHS, the national desire to honour the service of those who had lost their lives in the Second World War and create a fairer society for all is often identified as a key driver behind the Butler Act:

> the secondary stage will be designed, not only to provide an academic training for a select few, but to give equivalent opportunities to all children over 11, of making the most of their natural aptitudes [...] schools available for an area shall not be deemed to be sufficient unless they are sufficient in number, character, and equipment to afford for all pupils opportunities for education offering such variety of instruction and training as may be desirable in view of their different ages, abilities and aptitudes.
> (R.A. Butler speaking at the Second Reading of the Education Bill, 1944)

The Act drastically changed the landscape of schooling in Britain for three key reasons. It:

1. Exploded the number of students with which schools suddenly had to cope.
2. Dramatically transformed the demographic of young people who now required an education.
3. Created huge demands for new teachers, compounded by the already substantial depletion of trained professionals, a devastating number of whom had lost their lives in the Second World War.

2.6.1 New teachers, new students, new times

With the implementation of the Butler Act, individual Local Education Authorities (LEAs) were allowed to determine *how* they would provide this free secondary education for all. Most opted for a three-tier system, with different types of schools for different 'types' of students – grammar schools, secondary moderns and technical colleges – resonances of which still exist in some parts of the country today, such as Kent. The notable exception to this was London, which decided to opt for a comprehensive school system instead. This is where 'London English' gets its name. London English developed from the grassroots (by teachers themselves) largely through the creation of an organisation called LATE: the *London Association for the Teaching of English*. Gibbons explains:

> the old-style grammar school curriculum, devised for the relatively few so-called academic children, would simply not serve the many, and both established and newly trained English teachers lacked the tools with which to cope with the pupils now in front of them [...] This much was obvious to those who stood in front of the children in London, where comprehensive classrooms were a reality as early as the late 1940s
>
> (Gibbons 2017: 16).

Thus, the earlier incarnation of the subject came to be known as 'Cambridge English'. It was 'heavily influenced by F.R. Leavis [... and] placed canonical English literature at the centre of the curriculum and emphasised correctness in the use of spoken and written language' (Gibbons 2013: 1). The new model developed in response to the challenge of a comprehensive school system following the passing of the Butler Act, by contrast,

> grew from the work of academics and English teachers in the capital immediately after the war. Often referred to as a progressive model of English [... it] placed the child at the centre of the curriculum, valuing her experience and her language, and seeing the subject as linked to the development or growth of the individual within a social setting
>
> (Gibbons 2013: 1–2).

This sea change was borne out of a necessity to rapidly adapt to a vastly changed context for schools, teachers and students alike, but the persistence of 'Cambridge English' in some of the academically selective grammar schools in other parts of the country has bred an unfortunate characterisation over time that the latter is more rigorous and challenging; as better rather than different. This in turn has fostered and underpinned many later disputes, with at times an unfortunate emphasis on which model is right or better, rather than a more layered discussion about the intended purposes of particular content and what its inclusion aims to achieve. Somewhere along the way, arguments about appropriate content, pedagogies and different practical teaching activities became muddied and blurred, and all too often the three are lumped together when in reality they are distinct strands of consideration.

Ball and colleagues argue that the Cambridge and London models have caused a 'polarisation' within English education (1990: 57). However, Gibbons suggests this is a misleading simplification because it 'fails to take into account the relationship between the models and ignores the reality of the work of many English teachers' (2013: 2). Reflecting on the current diet of English in both schools and especially universities, there is clear force to Gibbons' point here, with elements of both Cambridge and London English being both present and valued in most institutions. Regardless of the reality, the idea of a strict choice between the two models remains a common conception and underpins many of the current major debates and conflicts around the subject.

2.7 Concerns about equity

A final key area informing conversations about the aims and purposes of English in general and studying fiction specifically are questions about equity in education. Which texts we choose to study has the potential to enfranchise some and disenfranchise others. To whom chosen texts appeal and what relevance they have to different student groups is another important consideration. Another common debate in this area focuses on whether there are consequences for individuals who are not familiar with certain works. All of these factors cannot easily be addressed simultaneously. For instance, choosing a novel that is of particular relevance to a cohort of

TABLE 2.1 A comparison of 'knowledge deficit' and 'critical pedagogy' views

The 'Knowledge Deficit' view	The 'Critical Pedagogy' view
A Key Figure: E. D. Hirsch Jr.	**A Key Figure:** Paulo Freire.
Identified 'problems' with the education system	
Lack of explicit knowledge teaching in schools is at the root of inequitable education.	Systemic structural inequity is at the root of inequitable education, which is reflected and perpetuated in schools.
An historic shift away from direct instruction is creating a 'knowledge deficit' for socially disadvantaged young people.	A middle-class curriculum is advantaging middle-class children, perpetuating and propping up wider inequity.
Diminishing prominence is being given to 'powerful' or 'core' knowledge disadvantaging those who do not naturally acquire it at home.	Difference is being wrongly viewed as deficit, treating students as empty vessels to be filled by their teachers, thus delegitimising the knowledge and experiences of some students.
Current 'progressive' approaches to education are causing or at least perpetuating inequity. Attainment gaps prove current approaches are not working.	Attainment gaps in school reflect wider social inequity: schools can (and must) help to redress this but not alone. It's unrealistic to expect schools to produce equal outcomes in an inequitable system.

students may well mean not teaching one we feel it is important for them to know about. Teacher specialisms derived from their own studies at university can also play a role in which texts they do and do not feel comfortable covering with their students. As such, just as with topics within English more broadly, texts can find themselves in competition with one another, and discussions can orient from what is an equitable English education to what is the most equitable choice a school or teacher can practically provide.

Activities and Reflections

1. What are your key priorities and concerns (and those of your department and school) relating to equitable education provision in relation to the study of fiction, and why?

Again, there are differing perspectives on what constitutes equity in the school, classroom and university. These broader positions inform the more microcosmic discussions about equitable education in English. To give a sense of how distinct these perspectives can be, Table 2.1 provides an outline of two, with Hirsch's philosophy broadly aligned with what might be termed 'traditionalist' views, and Freire, an oft invoked figure in relation to 'progressive' education.

Beliefs about the causes of inequity in education naturally inform the approaches schools and teachers adopt in trying to address it. Beliefs about the aims and purposes of education, in general or in relation to a particular subject, act as the foundation for what is designated as most important.

In the context of studying literature, the tensions between these two distinct conceptions of equitable education can be understood as a means of facilitating students' personal growth and skills of cultural analysis on the one hand, and an exercise in cultural heritage and accrual of cultural capital on the other. This divide could be characterised as respective emphases on engaging with and responding to texts against learning *content* (see Chapter 6 for more discussion). This tension is perhaps unsurprising when English education is situated within its historical context explored above.

2.7.1 The notion of literature as powerful knowledge

There has been a surge of support in the last few years from within the profession itself, championing a transmissive model of literature teaching focused explicitly on students accruing knowledge of certain texts. This has historically been a view more characteristic of policymakers than teachers. The influence of E. D. Hirsch is explicitly acknowledged (Hirsch et al. 1988). Hirsch's work focuses on the idea of 'core knowledge' and 'cultural literacy'. Hirsch defines being culturally literate as 'possess[ing] the basic information needed to thrive in the modern world' (Hirsch et al. 1988: xiii). Although offering a list of 5,000 'names, phrases, dates and concepts', which he argues constitutes this 'core knowledge', Hirsch contests the notion that this is prescriptive: 'cultural literacy is not represented by a prescriptive list of books but rather by a *descriptive* list of information actually possessed by literate Americans' (1988: xiv, emphasis in original). With regard to reading literature in particular he defends his list claiming:

> the idea of cultural literacy has been attacked by some liberals on the assumption that I must be advocating a list of great books that every child in the land should be forced to read […] very few specific titles appear on the list and they usually appear as words, not works, because they represent the writings that culturally literate people have read about but haven't read. *Das Kapital* is a good example.
>
> (Hirsch et al. 1988: xiv)

Hirsch's argument explicitly advocates in favour of a cultural heritage approach to teaching fiction, where learning discourse *about* texts is as good as, if not better than, young people actually reading them, and works that are 'known by the culturally literate' – predominantly canonical and 'the classics' – should form the exclusive focus of the English literature curriculum. It is important to recognise that this position not only downplays but further actively delegitimises the role of reading the text in the classroom *at all*, authentically or otherwise. The cultural literacy position has over time become associated with particular teaching methods, generally teacher-led didactic approaches where 'teacher is expert' and the main aim of lessons is to transmit knowledge about the class reader.

A useful metaphor with which to conceptualise the kinds of knowledge units championed by these positions is what Paulo Freire referred to as the 'banking metaphor' of education. Duncan-Andrade and Morrell (2008: 55) explain that under this paradigm:

> teachers treat students as passive, empty receptacles and schooling becomes a process whereby knowledgeable experts 'deposit' bits of information into the impoverished minds of students. Instead, Freire advocated a pedagogical practice centred upon dialogue, inquiry and the real exchange of ideas between teachers and students.

This deficit framing of the knowledge and experiences young people bring to the classroom, and the personal responses they provoke, is undoubtedly reflected in both Hirsch's language and his approach. Cultural literacy is presented as a relatively stable list with no recognition of other knowledge and experience. Whilst the positive intention regarding social justice is clear to see throughout Hirsch's writing, we would suggest that his approach codifies and perpetuates the very inequality he seeks to destroy by legitimising one form of knowledge and downgrading or dismissing others. At the same time, the questions of which knowledge is 'core', and which texts are the 'best that have been written' is a matter of both perspective and opinion. It is undoubtedly true that canonical texts – or 'the classics' – *are* currently imbued with a higher degree of cultural capital than, for example, the works of young adult authors such as Malorie Blackman or John Green. Yet, perhaps practitioners ought to reflect on why this is the case before committing large amounts of class time to making sure students learn about these 'great works' if it comes at the cost of meaningfully reading and engaging with others. We discuss some of these issues in more detail in Chapter 4.

> **Activities and Reflections**
>
> 1. What are your views on the positions taken by Hirsch and Freire?
> 2. How do these align with policies that exist in your department and school and those that form part of a wider national agenda in education?

Pedagogies oriented towards learning about, rather than authentically engaging with, texts may also encourage homogeneous and less creative responses from students. For example, Xerri (2013) draws on interviews with teachers and students to show how a vicious circle can operate in classrooms where teachers feel pressurised into providing 'meanings' of poems, and students are fearful of developing their own responses. In such a classroom, the teacher can be positioned as a 'gatekeeper to meaning' (135), with students often concerned with finding information *about* a poem rather than engaging in the clumsy and uncertain world of shaping and reshaping meaning through reading, discussion and re-reading. Consequently, there is a danger that practitioners lose sight of the importance of viewing reading as a transaction between text and reader where the reader's role as an active participant is foregrounded and knowledge is understood as negotiated and socially constructed (see for example discussion and associated pedagogies in Benton et al. 1988; Karolides 1999; Giovanelli 2016, 2017), rather than fixed as an element of knowledge, and transmitted. We return to these points throughout the remainder of this book, and specifically in Chapters 4 and 6.

Further reading

Simon Gibbons is an authority on the history of English education in the United Kingdom and English subject pedagogy more broadly. We would thoroughly recommend his work to anyone wishing to develop their knowledge of this area. Gibbons (2013) is an accessible entry point to his work; Gibbons (2014, 2017) both offer engaging longer treatments of this topic.

Bleiman (2020) is an excellent edited collection exploring the potential purposes of English teaching in general and studying fiction specifically. Eaglestone (2019) is a book-length reflection on the potential values of literary study. The cline of authentic and manufactured reading was first discussed in Giovanelli and Mason (2015) and elaborated in Mason and Giovanelli (2017). This chapter is in part based on these articles.

3
IDENTITY

This chapter will:

- reflect on the dynamics of different reading communities;
- offer a variety of ways of thinking about reading and readers in different contexts and spaces, including the English classroom;
- outline some key distinctions between first time reading and re-reading;
- explore the role power dynamics can play in conversations about a text;
- outline and analyse findings from the *Talking About Texts: Reading and Identity* project, an anonymous research questionnaire which investigated how we talk about books.

3.1 Reading in context

Stylistics and cognitive poetics both foreground the importance of considering reading as a practice which does not occur in a vacuum. Benwell explains how this approach to texts views 'reading as a socially situated, localised activity, contingent upon the context in which it is produced' (2009: 301). In other words, it is really important not to think about reading as one homogenous type of activity, but rather as something that we do in all different places and contexts for all sorts of different reasons. There are a variety of potential motivations to read, from wanting to relax or forget about a bad day for a few hours, to preparing to discuss what we have read with a class.

A person might read and, or, talk about the same book with a variety of different aims and goals at various points. Imagine, for a moment, an English teacher's possible interactions with a given text. The first time she began reading it, it was primarily to say that she had done so. She was in the staffroom speaking to a member of the Maths Department, who started talking about a book, and just assumed that the she had read it. The teacher bluffed her way through the conversation, but it felt embarrassing and threatening to her identity as a member of the English team, so after school, she went out and bought a copy, without much enthusiasm, but with a goal of safeguarding herself in future. However, by the time she is three quarters of the way through the book, the staffroom exchange is a distant memory. Now her main goal now is to find out 'whodunnit'. Six months later, the teacher's Head of Department announces that she will be teaching the book to Year 12. She reads it again, this time with the goal of designing and preparing a unit to teach. When she then reads it with the class (their first time, her third), the aim now is to immerse the students in the world of the text, hoping to recreate for them the same enjoyment the teacher felt when she read it for the first time herself. Next comes the revision lessons at the end of the year: at this point the teacher's main goal is to revisit important sections and help the students to try and memorise key quotations. Perhaps she even goes home at night and rereads the book hunting for any themes she might have missed that could show up on the exam.

This is an extended but not unrealistic scenario of one teacher's potential interactions with a book. The text has not changed, but the reader has, all because of context. The goals, intentions, joys and pressures, roles and responsibilities we adopt as readers can be highly fluid, and can all consciously and unconsciously influence the ways in which we read and what we might say, or not say, about a given text.

3.2 Studying fiction as a type of reading experience

Let's carry this forward to thinking about studying a fictional text in school. Here it is most useful to start with thinking about reading novels. This is because reading a novel in a classroom is both a highly familiar staple of school English, and an extremely odd type of reading experience, relative to almost any other, for both teachers and students. This is not just in terms of the actual way in which reading the text itself typically takes place, but also because of the identities everyone is asked to perform, as well as the perceived reasons for reading the book at all.

> **Activities and Reflections**
>
> 1. How and why might we read differently in English lessons, compared to purely for enjoyment?

First of all, thinking about other contexts in which reading and discussion of texts takes place – at a book group, socially with friends or strangers, curled up with the cat on the sofa, or for and then in a university seminar – it is very rare that people do both the reading and the discussion at the same time, or even move quickly between the two. Instead, in all these scenarios, it is generally the case that reading happens first, and talk later. By contrast, reading a novel in school English has systematically normalised the practice of interspersing actual reading with discussion and task completion, so much so that study editions of texts are sometimes physically sectioned with questions and tasks to be completed as the reader progresses through the text (for further discussion see Mason and Giovanelli 2017).

Second, it is also highly unusual for people within a group discussing a novel to be at dramatically different points in their reading of the text. Situations do arise every day where readers may begin discussing a book, only to discover that one of them has finished it whereas the other has not, but consider what typically happens then: readers will often engage in a checking procedure in order to establish whether they are both speaking from a similar point of text knowledge and, if an imbalance is discovered, will tend to either disengage from the conversation, or else carefully moderate what they say or hear, depending on which side of the imbalance they are on. Common phrases that readers might use in such scenarios include:

- "let's talk about it when you've finished"
- "where are you up to, what's happening at the moment?"

- "I'm just at the bit where…"
- "has anything happened [in this place/to this character/in relation to this topic]?"
- "no spoilers please!"
- "don't ruin it"

By contrast, in the classroom there can often be a significant imbalance in how much of the novel has been read, especially between teacher and students. This is not only normal, but usually actively expected: reading the book before teaching begins is considered a requirement of good professional practice. At the same time, most units are designed and run on the assumption that most students will not have read the book beforehand. In fact, it can often be viewed as a problem to have students in the class who are not encountering the text for the first time: how can they be stopped from revealing the big twist at the end, for example? In other words, if we consider teachers and their students not only as educators and learners, but also as readers, it becomes clear that prototypical course and lesson designs systematically and repeatedly ask first time readers and re-readers to interact in a manner people actively avoid in almost all other circumstances.

However, it is not universally the case that students must be first time readers of a text they study. Older students might, for instance, be asked to read the novel over their summer break before studying begins in the new term. Even in these scenarios, however, units are rarely delivered on the assumption that all students will in fact have done this as a result of the generally very sensible suspicion that at least some will not have done so, and this is a very difficult thing to prove. Equally, what of the students who have just transferred to the school and therefore did not know they were supposed to read certain texts? As such, pragmatism generally dictates that school courses that focus on studying a novel are not run in such a way as to effectively leave behind those individuals who didn't do as they were asked, or were not asked in the first place.

In higher education, this imbalance is, however, typically avoided, making studying fiction at this level in this respect more akin to booktalk in other scenarios. If the book in question is one which everyone is supposed to have read before the seminar or lecture, which is typically the case at least in UK universities, then students who don't finish in time are faced with a choice: go to class and risk finding out about the ending, or miss class and finish the book instead. Or there is an option to opt out of both reading and classes entirely. Or, for the very brave, there is the choice to attend the classes without having opened the novel at all and hope not to get caught out: it is well-documented that we can talk quite convincingly about books we have never read (see, for example, Bayard 2008), though it is uncontroversial to suggest that the odds of getting caught in your lie are substantially higher in a university seminar on the novel than they are in the course of chatting to a friend or even a stranger.

These are viable options for university students in a way that they are not for their younger peers in school, for several reasons. At university there is likely to be at least a degree of choice and optionality about which texts over the course of a module the student will ultimately be assessed on, so it is far easier to make such informed and strategic decisions both academically and personally: serving self-as-reader over self-as-student, and finishing the novel spoiler-free is a choice it is possible to make without dire consequence. Equally, the period for which classes focus on that particular novel are likely to be far, far shorter than the length of a unit studying a set text in earlier phases of education.

The same is not true in our secondary schools, and here English teachers in particular are faced with a problem: how does an educator, as a re-reader of a text, teach – or indeed talk at all – about a book which, for most of the course, the class hasn't read all the way through?

Third, there are few other contexts aside from the school English classroom where individual readers typically are not able to choose which text to read, or indeed to choose to stop reading a novel. This is described by Pennac as one of the fundamental 'rights of the reader': it is interesting to reflect on which of these rights are often not granted in the classroom:

- to not read
- to skip
- to not finish a book
- to read it again
- to read anything
- to mistake a book for real life
- to read anywhere
- to dip in
- to read out loud
- to be quiet

(Pennac 1992)

Activities and Reflections

1. Do you agree with all of Pennac's 'rights'?
2. Would you change any?

This is not to suggest that Pennac's manifesto is an empirically tested study of how reading should be, in the classroom or anywhere else. Nor is this to say all of these features are necessarily desirable in the context of studying a text. Nor even that some of these 'rights' are always realistically actionable in a lesson: it is hard, for example, to envisage a way in which a teacher might give multiple students in the same room, reading the same text at the same time, the right to read out loud and the right to be quiet. Equally, the realities of our assessment systems fundamentally problematise granting students 'the right not to read' the specific texts they've been assigned, let alone at all. Nonetheless, Pennac's list has enjoyed enduring and widespread popularity: it has been in circulation since 1992 (originally in French) and has since sold millions of copies, been translated into a host of different languages, and even been turned into a poster illustrated by the famous children's illustrator, Quentin Blake. This suggests an endorsement of these proposed rights at least in certain contexts, and this does raise important questions:

1. How closely aligned should studying fiction and reading for pleasure be?
2. Does it matter if these two types of reading experience are very different?
3. Could studying fiction be realistically aligned to more closely resemble reading in other contexts and, if so, what would the potential advantages and disadvantages be?
4. If readers are not afforded the same rights in the classroom as they are in the rest of their lives, then what is studying fiction for, and why is it being taught and studied in this way?

We suggest that these are powerful and important questions for the field of English education to contemplate, because they involve reflection on both the core values of studying fiction and, crucially, consideration of the relationship between our beliefs and what we consider good and desirable practices. This is vital because there are several different potential responses to the question why do we study fiction, and they do not all sit in complement with one another in terms of how they inform the priorities that are then enacted in individual classrooms. To explore these questions, we now step back to consider some of the key sociological factors that influence us when we read, discuss and think about fiction. We will then return to some of the key conceptions of the value of studying works of fiction with young people outlined in Chapter 2, and consider the different versions of reading in the English classroom they champion.

Activities and Reflections

1. Ask your students why they think they study texts (or the particular text you are currently reading with them) in English. What do they think the reasons are? Can you see where these ideas have come from? How closely do they align with your own feelings about the purposes for reading?
2. Discuss the four questions above with your colleagues: how closely does your curriculum design reflect your beliefs and responses? Given the opportunity, is there anything about your unit or lesson designs you would change based on your discussion?

3.3 Booktalk and power

Booktalk (referring to the ways we talk about books), just like any other interaction, necessarily involves power dynamics operating between participants. In this chapter so far, we have identified several factors that can determine whether readers are more or less powerful participants (Fairclough 2014). Notably the power people have in the course of booktalk is not always exercised, and the dynamics that unfold in the course of a discussion may not always match the reality of a dynamic but rather participants' perceptions of them. These include, for example:

- **Role in the space:** teachers will typically have more power than students in a school or classroom (sometimes referred to as a 'category entitlement' (Potter 1996; Peplow 2011)).
- **Text knowledge:** readers who have finished a book will typically have more power than readers who are part way through. Individuals who have read some of a book will typically have more power than those who have read none of it.
- **Perceived/assumed text knowledge:** individuals who successfully present themselves as being knowledgeable about the text will tend to have power, regardless of whether this is knowledge they genuinely possess.
- **Topic expertise:** power is typically afforded to people who have expertise in a particular topic, for instance an identified theme, discussed in the course of booktalk. This expertise might be experiential or academic, though these sources may be afforded different weights depending on the topic and the context.
- **Perceived/assumed topic expertise:** individuals who successfully present as being knowledgeable about a topic will tend to be powerful participants whether or not they are being truthful.

- **Perceived/assumed literary expertise:** what constitutes literary expertise is highly contested, however individuals who successfully present as having it, whether that be through qualification, role, or being deemed as knowledgeable about literature in general, will tend to be powerful participants whether or not they are being truthful.

Power dynamics in any conversation will also inevitably be affected by the degree of social closeness or distance between members of the group, and this is not always linear or obvious to determine (Brown and Levinson 1982). We could reasonably assume, for example, that there would be a wider degree of social distance between a teacher and student than between lifelong friends, with two members of the same reading group somewhere in the middle. However, a plethora of often unknowable variables can easily invert many of these assumptions: one friend might be secretly intimidated by the other; a normally excellent rapport between student and teacher may be affected by the presence of another student in the class, for instance. That said, just because all the relevant context affecting what people may or may not feel confident to say is not easy to establish, it does not stop it from being valuable to reflect on.

3.3.1 Power and identity

One aspect of studying fiction where carefully considering the potential influence of power dynamics is of particular value is in relation to personal response. Even if the responses students are being asked to generate do not seem objectively that 'personal' or sensitive, it is worth thinking about such requests through the lens of identity. Parroting back something a teacher has already covered is far less identity exposing, or indeed threatening for a student than offering their own thoughts. Turner (1968) discusses this in terms of 'self-conception' and 'self-images'. He explains that identity comprises two closely linked aspects. The first, self-conception, is our more enduring and stable sense of who we are. Self-images, by contrast, are the day-to-day, sometimes moment-to-moment inputs we get through our interactions with the world around us, which can either confirm and reinforce our self-conception, or alternatively challenge or even upset it. Mason (2019: 104) explains the relationship between the two, situating this model in the context of education:

> Whilst self-conception is the more stable aspect of our sense of our own identity, Turner argues that it can be altered by the self-images we encounter, whether dramatic moments which disrupt our self-conception at a fundamental level – the aspiring lawyer who *knows* they will be the next Clarence Darrow failing the final exam – or the more subtle erosion over an extended period – the student who defines themselves by their superior intelligence who transitions to university and repeatedly struggles to achieve in every class. In both instances, the individual's sense of who they are in this particular aspect of their lives – in this case academic – is potentially changed and reshaped by their interactions with their environment.

As Turner explains, 'each person's self-conception is a selective working compromise between [their] ideals and the images forced upon [them] by [their] imperfect behaviour in actual situations' (1968: 94). As such, there are multiple aspects of a student's self-conception that may make them nervous or indeed unwilling to share their personal responses in a classroom environment for fear of experiencing self-images that disrupt this preferred version of themselves. These may range from conceptions that focus on academics, such as 'I think of myself as good at English and I'm worried this is wrong', to those relating to reading like 'I don't want to be thought of as a reader so I won't say anything', to even those more broadly relating to personal qualities like 'I don't think of myself as emotional, and speaking will reveal this has affected me'.

These same identity pressures can also weigh heavily on teachers, especially teachers of English, who are likely to find classroom interactions that reinforce their self-conception as a 'good teacher' pleasurable and positive, and those that may threaten that conception, such as being asked to teach something unfamiliar, threatening and anxiety provoking. Giovanelli (2015) investigated exactly this phenomenon in relation to teachers with backgrounds in literature being asked to teach A-level English Language for the first time. He found that this task presented challenging, even terrifying, self-images to the teachers in his study, whose professional identity was then put in jeopardy. Over time, however, as the teachers developed their knowledge of language and linguistics and began to relish teaching these new topics, these self-images transformed their self-conception, and broadened out their sense of what it meant for them to be an English teacher in a positive and rewarding way.

Activities and Reflections

1. How do the self-images you encounter in your day-to-day teaching reinforce or threaten your self-conception? Do you feel you enact different aspects of your identity when teaching different topics?
2. Reflecting on your own times as a student, what role did your interactions with educational spaces play in shaping your current sense of identity?

The next part of this chapter now builds on these ideas, reporting the findings of an empirical study on reading and identity, focusing specifically on English teachers and reading.

3.4 *Talking About Texts: Reading and Identity* Project – an overview

The *Talking About Texts: Reading and Identity* project ran in the summer of 2019. It comprised an anonymous online questionnaire which was predominantly distributed on the social networking site, *Twitter*. Around two thirds of the respondents worked in education, and nearly half were teachers, which makes it of particular interest and relevance here.

The questionnaire asked participants questions such as:

- Have you ever read and enjoyed a book you'd be reluctant to tell others about?
- Are there any circumstances in which you might lie about reading a book you hadn't read?
- Do you ever feel embarrassed about books you haven't read?

As the survey was anonymous, participants had no need to worry about the impact their answers may have on how they were viewed. *Talking About Texts* aimed to delve into an aspect of booktalk as central and prescient as it is taboo: lying about our reading. In recent years, stylistics and cognitive poetics has experienced a turn towards examining the words of real readers, in reviews and exchanges with one another, as a means of better understanding their thinking processes and responses. However, much of this work passively assumes that readers are honest in their representations of their thoughts, feelings, tastes and knowledge of the texts they discuss. This research therefore aimed to add socio-cultural and contextual nuance to this body of work, by asking readers to reflect on factors that may inform what they do and do not say in the course of booktalk. The rest of this chapter will explore its findings and reflect on what these may mean for English and its teachers.

> **Activities and Reflections**
>
> 1. You can find a full copy of the *Talking About Texts: Reading and Identity* questionnaire in the Appendix of this book. Read through and consider what your own answers to the questions would be. You could use some of these topics or questions as the basis of a discussion task with your class.
> 2. What's the most famous text you've never read? Do you care?

3.4.1 Who participated in Talking About Texts?

653 people participated in the *Talking About Texts* project, ultimately yielding 644 valid responses. As an anonymous survey, the information available about who the participants were is necessarily limited, reduced to three questions, two of which were asked at the end of the survey after participants had already answered the substantive questions. The survey was also divided into sections so later questions were not visible whilst earlier ones were completed. The three pieces of information requested about the respondents themselves were:

1. Q7: Would you call yourself a reader?
2. Q19: Roughly how many books do you read in an average year?
3. Q22: How would you best describe your job or profession (this can be a current or previous role)?

The first question – would you call yourself a reader – was asked for two reasons. One, because it informs all of the other responses, the question asked participants whether this was an identity they claimed for themselves or not. Two, the vast majority of existing research on talking about texts focuses on people who it is reasonable to assume do self-identify as readers, either because they are the group the researcher is interested in (see, for example, Cliff-Hodges 2010) or more often simply because these people naturally populate the spaces being researched, from book groups (for example Hartley 2001) to online review sites (for example Nuttall 2015, 2017; Harrison and Nuttall 2019). Simply put, people who either do not identify as readers, or who even actively identify as "not a reader" are a much harder to reach population. As such, it was felt that an anonymous context might be one of the few ways in which to capture the voices of this group, and therefore if they were present, it was important to know. Interestingly in and of itself, whilst the survey was advertised as open to anyone to complete, 'non-readers' still made up less than 5% of participants (see Figure 3.1):

This in itself merits reflection. It may be that a survey called *Talking About Texts* simply holds no interest or appeal for most people who do not themselves identify as a reader. It may also be that there is something inherently identity-threatening for non-readers about being asked to discuss

28 Identity

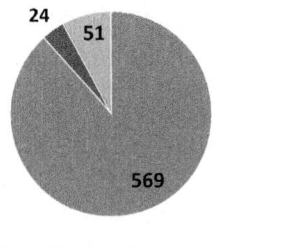

Pie chart showing: 569, 51, 24

■ Yes (88.3%)   ■ No (3.7%)   ■ It depends (7.9%)

FIGURE 3.1 Responses to Q7: Would you call yourself 'a reader'?

reading and identity. This may also have been a result of the questionnaire's design. The first substantive question asked (following those ensuring active consent) was 'What is your favourite book? (You can list up to three if you can't decide)'. This was intended as a low-stakes way in which to focus participants' thinking on their own reading tastes and practices, but may inadvertently have been off-putting to non-readers, as this is arguably a question which addresses 'readers'. As there is no way to gauge how many people began the survey and then clicked off it, it is impossible to assess whether this was the case. Nonetheless, it seems unlikely that this last explanation alone would account for the stark absence of non-readers, and thus it may be useful for educators wishing to engage students in discussions about literature to be mindful that those who do not identify as readers may enter these conversations already with a sense that these topics are not 'for' them.

The second and third demographic questions did not appear until the end of the survey, and so unlike the first, almost certainly did not impact who completed it. It is of course possible that some participants failed to complete the survey and closed it upon reaching these questions. Again, as it is the best way to enact participants ethical 'right to withdraw' in an online context, this data would not have been captured. However, it is reasonable to assume that having invested time in completing the survey (the average completion took 22 minutes) most people would not abandon it that near the end, and the survey did indicate to participants how far through they were at each stage.

The second question – 'Roughly how many books do you read in a year?' – was asked because the researcher (Mason) hypothesised that how much a person reads likely plays a central role in determining how they feel about the topics they were being asked about, and if it proved not to, that this would also be an important finding. In other words, it seems intuitively logical that how much we read affects how we talk about texts, and if it doesn't this would also be extremely valuable to know. The distribution of how many books participants reported to read in an average year is shown in Figure 3.2.

Again, this is noteworthy in and of itself. 273 of the participants, 42%, reported reading more than 25 books per year, more than one a fortnight. Nearly two thirds of participants (64%) read more than a book a month at 16 or over. There is no average of the general population to compare this to, and as this very likely varies from country to country and nationality of participants was not captured making such comparisons would still be difficult. However, this is very high when considering that Nielson Book Research (2019) claims only 10% of adults are 'heavy readers', defined as those who purchase 16 or more books a year. This is therefore important to bear in mind when considering the trends and themes in the other responses: by any sensible assessment at least two thirds of the people who engaged in this research spend a lot of their time reading. It is also worth contemplating why this skew in the demographics may have arisen. Could it

19. Roughly, how many books do you read in an average year? (Remember you can include audio books and books you've read on an e-reader)

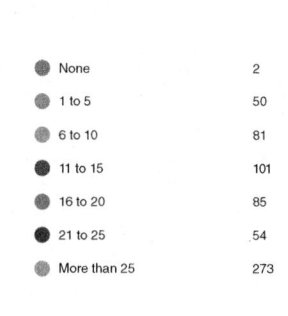

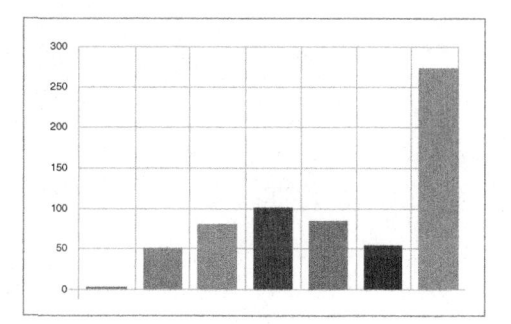

None	2
1 to 5	50
6 to 10	81
11 to 15	101
16 to 20	85
21 to 25	54
More than 25	273

FIGURE 3.2 Books read per year reported by respondents to the *Talking About Texts* survey

be, for instance, that people need to spend a lot of their time reading in order to feel confident to complete this kind of survey, even if it's anonymous? Do people who read a lot find reflecting on reading practices more interesting?

The third and final demographic question, 'how would you best describe your job or profession? (This can be a current or previous role)', was asked because the interaction between reading, identity and education was a particular interest of the research. Even without this interest, however, a person's job – how they spend much of their time – seems pertinent to any investigation of identity. Specifically, anyone working in a role that directly involves talking about texts may well have a different perspective from someone who does not. This therefore seemed vital information to gather. Note the framing of the question allowed participants to describe this aspect of themselves however they wished (rather than, for instance, having to select a 'best fit' from a drop-down list). The question was formatted in this way because, as a survey about identity, it seemed appropriate to facilitate participants in expressing this important aspect of themselves in a way they felt was accurate and in a manner over which they had total control. People from all manner of roles engaged in the *Talking About Texts* study, from those who identified as unemployed or retired to stay-at-home mothers, from carers, barristers and surgeons to probation officers, and one participant who delightfully just wrote 'ambulance man'. A large proportion of respondents, however, worked in education, most commonly teachers and academics (of all subjects, but especially English). Table 3.1 shows the breakdown of the participants by profession:

This strong representation of participants working in education is entirely expected, and in this instance can be easily explained by the avenues through which the project was disseminated. The questionnaire was primarily advertised on two Twitter accounts, the researcher's own (@DrofletJess) and another account belonging to the researcher that is attached to

TABLE 3.1 Professions of *Talking About Texts* participants

Teachers	296
Academics	102
Education: Other	87
Librarians	10
Other	149
Total	**644**

a final year undergraduate module 'Exploring English Education' (@ExploringEngEd) at Sheffield Hallam University which, as the name suggests, focuses on English education. The key tweet used to promote the study made no mention of education or teachers. However, being shared on these platforms will have naturally meant it was disproportionately visible to these groups. The tweet was shared widely and will therefore have been drawn to the attention of a broad range of people: just the initial tweet was shared (retweeted) 178 times and seen by over 52,000 Twitter users. Prominent amongst users who helped distribute *Talking About Texts* were several people and organisations who also work in the field of English education, thus further increasing the likelihood of the sample being skewed toward this group. This included groups such as Team English (a grassroots powerhouse of English teachers with over 29,000 followers at the time of writing), the *National Association for the Teaching of English* (NATE), and the *English Media Centre* (EMC), as well as noted author and Professor of Children's Literature, Michael Rosen. This strong representation of such professionals, and especially teachers, allows us to explore the relationship between reading and identity in perhaps the most important context: education.

3.4.2 Talking About Texts: Key information about participants, an overview

To briefly summarise the key information from the previous section about the individuals who participated in *Talking About Texts*, then:

- the survey was anonymous
- the survey ran between July and September 2019
- 644 people participated
- 88% of participants said that yes, they would call themselves 'a reader'
- 42% of participants said that they read more than 25 books a year
- just under half of participants (46%) identified themselves as teachers
- three quarters of participants (75%) identified themselves as working in some sort of role in the education sector
- the survey was mainly disseminated on the social media site Twitter

3.5 'As a teacher': reading and professional identity

A prevalent theme within the responses from educators is the invocation of a professional identity in the contemplation of reading and their sense of embarrassment or confidence, judgement, and the expectations from others. There are, for instance, 38 instances of the phrase 'as an English teacher' present in the data, and a further 12 of 'as a teacher'. As an adverbial phrase, this is not syntactically necessary, but rather functions to provide additional information. That is, these participants are choosing to add this qualifying detail to their responses, positioning themselves as speaking from or through this particular aspect of their identity. There are numerous uses of similar phrases, including 'I teach [English]' and 'I am an [English teacher]'(not in response to 'What's your job?'!), also being used to qualify or explain an adjacent comment, as well as different ways in which individuals have expressed the same sentiment, like Participant 514, who wrote: 'in my profession you are expected to be well read. I am much younger than my colleagues and I feel this works against me in this aspect.' Similarly, asked if there were any circumstances in which they might lie and say they had read a book when then hadn't, Participant 523 simply answered, 'frequently! Occupational hazard.' Almost universally, these phrases and comments accompany either expressions of inadequacy, or identification of expectations

```
                them! Embarrassed is perhaps the wrong word, but as an English teacher and voracious reader my impo
                         Some classics I feel I should have read as an English teacher As an English teacher I
                              and I read as part pf my job as an English teacher. As an English teacher there
                        like I should have read all the classics as an English teacher. Because as an English teach
                    probably should have read but haven't! Yes! As an English teacher, everyone expects you to kno
                 ery opinionated about what is good literature and as an English teacher I am expected by others
                  They are pulpy and not particularly well-written. As an English teacher I feel I should read
              stantly reading more advanced fiction? Yes, again as an English teacher I feel I am expected
                    rather than just reading books that I teach As an English teacher I feel I should have
                        teacher, I'll never have read widely enough! As an English teacher I feel I am expected
                     all the classics as an English teacher. Because as an English teacher I feel I am expected
                          you think should fill There are classics which as an English teacher I feel I should have
                             and no reading is bad reading. Just enjoy! As an English teacher I feel like I should
```

FIGURE 3.3 Concordance snapshot for the phrase 'as an English teacher', sorted alphabetically by words to the right

surrounding the individual's reading history and practices, often both. Figure 3.3 shows a snapshot of the concordance (a lined up collection of the instances of a particular word or phrase) of 'as an English teacher'. The concordance was generated using *AntConc* (Anthony 2014) software.

What is particularly notable here is that none of the uses of this phrase section off being 'an English teacher' as one aspect of their identity, but instead appear to encompass the identity stance being adopted. This sense is strengthened by the frequent use of the first-person pronoun 'I' as an alternative self-referential naming strategy, linguistically suggesting an equivalence between them. This resonates with Goodwyn's (2002) study, which found that around 75% of trainee English teachers cite being a lover of reading as their primary reason for their career choice. In other words, for many English, teachers their professional identity seems largely inseparable from their personal one. This raises pressing questions about how this positions English teachers whose academic background is not in literature.

Activities and Reflections

1. Given that English teachers are recruited a diverse range of degree backgrounds, should non-literature trainees be forewarned or prepared for the incipient expectation that they will be 'lovers of reading', or should we be challenging this stereotype?
2. Apart from being a 'lover of reading', what alternative or additional positive 'English teacher identities' could there be?
3. Is it possible to escape the expectation that English teachers all love reading? If not, is this a problem? Why? Why not?

Equally susceptible to these feelings of inadequacy are teachers whose background is simply not in the 'right kind of literature', like Participant 319, who shared:

> As an English teacher who did a degree in Spanish and Portuguese, which was literature heavy, I have a different reading background to many other English teachers. I often worry

about my reading history being inadequate and feel embarrassed that I might not know as much as others.

Even more concerningly, this comment is reflected in many others from participants of other or additional cultural backgrounds. Participant 112, an academic who reads more than 25 books a year stated, 'I haven't read some of the classics because I grew up in a different country and the canon was different'. Participant 241, who reads 6 to 10 books a year and describes their profession as 'roles in education, including teacher and published author'. expands, saying:

In the UK, for example where I'm born and live, you're expected to have read certain classics which I would find very very boring. I've tried reading them and hate them. But this poses amongst the educated as they expect you've just read and understand these books. However, if your cultural capital is a lot wider, (I am ethnically not white British), then you draw on books, plays and poetry from other cultures which mean more to you – however these aren't recognised.

This participant's invocation of 'cultural capital' may well be reflective of the rise of discussions around this very topic on 'Edutwitter' (the name commonly given to the community of individuals interested in education on Twitter): this is the platform on which the study was primarily disseminated and the eight instances of this phrase are made exclusively by participants whose profession is situated in education.

Positively, the number of these comments are matched by those of participants problematising a lack of diversity in their own reading histories and practices. For instance:

- There are lots of books I think I should read and it's impossible to fit them all in. I feel embarrassed not to have read more by women of colour. (Participant 466)
- I own more books than I have read, I feel lazy. I don't read enough books by women or by people of colour. I feel poorly read but superficially well informed about books. (Participant 601)
- I feel as though I haven't read with enough breadth to understand the world enough. (Participant 337)

Some of these comments are accompanied by statements about the participant's aspirations to address these perceived gaps, and whilst aspirations are not, of course, action, it is positive to see. It is possible that the majority of participants do read diversely and thus felt no need to mention this at all. Yet, in England at least, we face a curriculum at Key Stages 4 and 5 (ages 14–18) that increasingly and deliberately focuses on 'English' texts (geographically speaking), especially those written before 1900 (and thus, largely inheriting all the lack of ethnic and cultural diversity characteristic of the period). In this context we might ask what professional incentive teachers are being offered to broaden their reading choices. If the curriculum is doing anything, is it not in fact encouraging teachers to narrow their reading to focus on a specific group of texts, the so-called British canon or 'the classics'? And if teachers from other cultures feel this way, that the texts from their own culture are better and more interesting, but 'aren't recognised' and therefore don't count, is it not reasonable to suspect that students from other cultures may feel the same? This leads onto the next stark theme that emerged from the *Talking About Texts* project.

3.6 Lying about reading, and what it means for English

Participants were asked, 'Are there any circumstances in which you might lie about reading a book you hadn't read?' The question allowed an open narrative response with a further opportunity to elaborate on any specific titles and why they gave their initial answer. 38.6% said Yes, and 59.9% said No, with a final small minority of responses that were so ambiguous it was impossible to categorise them as either. Thus, a significant minority of participants would lie and pretend to have read a book when they hadn't. Bearing in mind the demographic makeup of the participants, most of whom think of themselves as readers, and a majority of whom both work in education and read upwards of 16 books a year, this says something about the powerful weight of social pressures to appear well read. If this many teachers feel compelled to maintain these kinds of pretences, what does it suggest about students? Does this suggest, perhaps, that we are tacitly communicating that being 'good' at English means having read everything?

When unravelling the narrative responses qualifying these statistics, a clear pattern emerges of distinctions being made between what might best be termed 'active' and 'passive' lying, with disagreement amongst participants about what actually counts. Many of those who placed themselves into the 'No' category, for instance, described behaviours they did engage in such as staying quiet, being evasive, nodding along, withdrawing from a conversation and giving the impression or allowing the assumption that they had read something, which they did not feel escalated to the threshold of 'actually lying'.

Similarly, in response to the question 'Do you ever feel embarrassed about books you haven't read?' 45.8% of the participants said Yes and 54.2% said No. Again, this suggests that even amongst this group of people, who one might reasonably anticipate would feel the most confident and secure in their reading identity, concerns about perceived 'gaps' or 'deficits' in their reading were able to prompt an emotion as powerful as embarrassment.

Activities and Reflections

1. What role does identity play in the conversations that unfold in the course of studying fiction, for both teachers and their students? It may be productive to choose a lesson or unit you have recently taught and reflect on it through this lens.
2. Can feelings like embarrassment and fear of judgement be tackled in the literature classroom? If so, is it better to acknowledge or try to mitigate these emotions?

3.6.1 Growing into confidence?

Closer examination of the narrative responses of those participants who stated that they were either not embarrassed about books they had not read, or wouldn't say that they had read something when in fact they had not revealed an interesting and prevalent theme. Many of these individuals qualified that this was not something they felt or something that they would do *anymore*. Many recognised these behaviours as something they would, however, have done when they were younger. In most cases participants attributed this change in mindset to either having grown in confidence or now being old enough to no longer care. Here are some examples. All of these participants are teachers:

- I've read a huge number of books, and used to think that as it's such a part of my life both in and outside of work, I should have read all the classics and also keep up to date with the

latest releases. After my fourth or fifth attempt to re-read Wuthering Heights a few years ago I decided life's too short, and there are too many good books, to waste time being worried about books that just aren't for me (Participant 559).
- I used to lie at university when students who had been to private schools or grammar schools listed canonical texts that I hadn't read. Most frequently this was things like a Pride and Prejudice or Great Expectations. I read these books later as an adult but at the time I felt embarrassed and so nodded along (Participant 398).
- I used to feel this way about some of the classics, when I was a younger teacher and felt I might be judged about not having been as widely read. As I got more experienced, I realised that I had read lots of books that others hadn't and stopped caring! (Participant 130).
- When I was younger but I'm too old to care (Participant 310).
- I'm too old to give a damn (Participant 147).

In other words, these confident and assured adult readers speak of successfully graduating out of their worry and embarrassment about all the things they feel they should have read.

How many young people just give up on reading instead? The findings discussed above have some implications for young readers and their identities. Given that many of the adults spoke about their anxiety over reading, or not reading, certain books, it seems reasonable to suggest that students also experience these worries and concerns, perhaps to an even stronger degree. This seems to be reinforced by comments from teachers above who narrate a journey of becoming confident carefree readers through an incremental process of caring less and less about the opinions and potential judgements of others. As such, the role of identity appears to be a factor which merits serious consideration in every aspect of studying fiction.

Further reading

Peplow (2011) offers an insightful analysis of the ways in which identity can affect booktalk in reading groups, with particularly relevant discussion of the notion of 'expertise'. Allington (2011, 2012) and Whiteley (2011a, 2011b) also undertake useful research in this area, with the former focusing on group make up and dynamics and the latter on the role of emotions. Any work by Gabrielle Cliff-Hodges will be of interest to readers interested in topics covered in this chapter. In particular, Cliff-Hodges (2010) examines the discourse and characteristics of young people who do identify as readers.

4
TEXT CHOICES

This chapter will:

- outline the key debates that have historically surrounded the question of which texts young people should formally study;
- consider the practical constraints that can limit and inform the choices we make about which texts to study;
- reflect on potential advantages and disadvantages of different criteria we employ when choosing a text;
- offer ways of conceiving 'challenge' in relation to text choice;
- introduce the concept of 'narrative schemas'.

4.1 Decisions, decisions

There are several ongoing debates around studying fiction in school including, but not limited to:

- How many texts should students study?
- From what era?
- By which authors?
- From which countries?
- To what end?
- Should exams be open or closed book?
- Should English be assessed using coursework?
- What's the best pedagogical approach when studying texts?

However, one of the most ferocious and divisive issues relating to this particular aspect of the curriculum invariably comes down to debates around text choice: which specific texts should students read, and why? In this chapter, whilst we will not shy away from the reality that ultimately decisions about text choice have to be made in and for any classroom, we will argue that the polarising way in which this discussion is typically framed: pitting texts and genres against one another as though one choice is universally 'right' and the other 'wrong', is both unhelpful and unnecessary.

36 Text choices

It is not possible to study every book that has ever been written with students. We couldn't read all of these books in a single lifetime even if we were so inclined, could read at super human speeds and did nothing else but! As such, in our own lives each book we choose to read, or not to read, can feel (and be) a meaningful decision. Each book we mentally shelve on our 'read' list takes a space another now cannot, and the length of the shelf is finite, though we don't know how much room remains. At the same time, it is well known that reading a text that particularly resonates can be a hugely powerful experience that reverberates through every aspect of a person's life (see, for example Gerrig 1993; Green and Brock 2000; Stockwell 2009; Whiteley 2011a, 2011b; Alsup 2015). In his study of the reading histories of trainee English teachers, Goodwyn (2002) finds that most of the individuals in his study had just such an experience with a text during their adolescent years. He explains, 'for most of these readers there is at least one vividly powerful memory of reading a text whose effect is so great that things are changed [...] the text demands that they think again, that they change, even that they must try to effect change in the world' (Goodwyn, 2002: 73). Gerrig (1993) similarly examines the potential impact of authentic reading in terms of the power of a highly immersive text. Describing the sensation of 'getting lost in a book' through the metaphor of reader as traveller and text as another world, Gerrig explains how travellers can return to their real lives 'changed by the journey'. One text rather than another can be the difference between a young person deciding whether or not they 'are a reader'. The experience of studying a particular text can breed and foster associations with reading more broadly, associations to everything from enjoyment and curiosity to dislike or even fear.

It is unsurprising, then, that discussions about text choice often quickly turn to the question of opportunity cost: it is not just the choice of a particular text, it is also the text that cannot now be taught as a result of choosing the other one. It is also not surprising that such debates often centre on the study of fiction specifically, rather than another aspect of the English curriculum, simply because of the relatively large chunk of time such units typically require. If it were somehow possible to study a different text, in full, every single lesson, most arguments about the relative values of an extra Shakespeare play or Louis Sachar's YA novel *Holes* would all but disappear.

At the root of these debates is this very question of relative value, and at the root of that are a variety of different ideological positions within the English education community about what studying fiction is 'for'. What we actually want to achieve through the act of reading and studying texts with young people is a discussion not often had, but one which underpins and informs almost every debate that flows forward from it. Investigating the possible purposes of set texts will form the focus of the second half of the chapter. First, however, we will pause to consider some of the practical parameters that inform decisions about text choices.

4.2 Practical parameters

Whilst debates rage about the relative value of particular works, many texts are excluded from the conversation entirely. This is typically because they simply aren't viewed as viable choices, by anyone, regardless of their other views. Very long texts, for example, never form part of the discussion because of the length of time they would take a class to get through, especially in schools where all or most of the actual reading is expected to take place in lessons. This is in spite of the fact that we know many young people will sit down to read lengthy tomes in certain circumstances: Tolkien's *The Lord of the Rings* and J K Rowling's *Harry Potter and the Order of the Phoenix* come in at 1,244 and 766 pages respectively. Practitioners and researchers tend not to debate the potential merits of studying *The Stand* or *It* by Stephen King, or indeed *War and Peace*, because all three are over a thousand pages, and everyone agrees that this would not be sensible. So, there are hardlines and points of agreement within these debates, even from those otherwise at polar opposite ends of the spectrum on other aspects of the issue. One must wonder, therefore, whether Shakespeare's place in the curriculum would have ever been attained if each of his plays was ten hours long. Would none of us have ever studied Shakespeare, or would schools have reconceived of what it means to study a text? Are there tacit conditions for a text being worthy of study that pass below the field of our attention?

Another practical issue for schools is the financial imposition of purchasing a large number of copies of the same text. Realistically, choices are often limited to what is available in the cupboards. This can mean that the longevity of a text choice decision can range into decades.

Economic constraints on choices in education are unlikely to be a revelation to anyone reading this book, but the degree to which this issue bleeds into so many aspects of text choice is understated. In some schools it has been engrained practice to study the same text with a particular year group for generations, meaning teachers can even end up teaching a text they themselves studied at school. It is worth noting that the rise of teachers on social media has offered new ways to facilitate text changes, for example through online swap shops; however, this practice remains far from common. As such, what may well have simply begun as a financial constraint can spawn a number of by-products that sustain that text choice for years to come, from the bank of resources built up in the department, to the reliable track record of exam success, to teachers' feelings of comfort, confidence, or even simple affection for that particular text. In other words, once a text choice is embedded within a department it garners many incentives to keep it there.

Activities and Reflections

1. Think back to when you or your department last chose to stop studying a particular text and/or start studying a new one. What thinking underpinned the decisions?

Another constraint at particular stages in education relates to which texts are available on the examination specifications. It would be naïve, however, to suggest that questions about budgets, resources and workload do not also impinge on choice even here, which raises questions about when and where changes to available text choices for a school are actually meaningful. If an awarding body decides to put a brand-new contemporary text onto a specification, this does not mean a school can afford to buy in copies of it. This is not just because of the burden of the bulk purchase itself, but also the simple market reality that new, popular books cost a lot more than reprints of old favourites. Is one of the reasons we tend to study Charlotte Bronte's *Jane Eyre* rather than Johnathan Saffer Foer's *Extremely Loud and Incredibly Close* actually nothing to do with the former being pedagogically more worthy, and everything to do with the latter being five times the price?

Departments also have to decide if students are allowed to take copies of the book home to read and work with. There are sometimes stark contrasts between schools' practices which can reflect and exaggerate the relative affluence of the area the school serves. In some places it can be a reasonable request to ask families to buy their children copies of their GCSE texts, for example, where in others this would simply not be feasible, realistic or fair to request. This question of access to texts permeates decisions about choice too, since a book that cannot be taken home cannot be read at home, pushing the pressure to dedicate time to actual reading into the classroom, potentially making the selection of shorter texts a practical necessity.

Another key issue to consider is individual teachers' and the department's levels of confidence with a particular text. As will be discussed more expansively in the later parts of this chapter, all text choices are not created equal in this regard. It would be interesting, for instance, to know how many staple choices of the literature curricula around the world are being taught by people who studied those books themselves, whether at school or university. The notion of teaching a work, author, genre or period with which you are wholly unfamiliar can be an understandably daunting one. It is easy to see why teachers may choose to avoid such texts if given the option, especially in a context where it is readily apparent that workloads, accountability and stress levels are often unacceptably high.

Other constraints might include whether a teacher feels confident perhaps not with the text but with navigating the content of the discussions that may arise in lessons as a result. This issue can influence decisions around teaching approach as much as text choice. It is one thing to promote the idea of studying fiction that opens up important conversations around topics such as race, gender and mental health; it is quite another to support, train and equip teachers to feel confident to lead and manage those conversations with a room full of young people. Without the latter, any attempt at the former is ultimately disingenuous. These are not quick fix or one-dimensional issues. To meaningfully undertake the study of fiction with a view to engaging students in critical reflection of difficult and sensitive topics requires far more than simply choosing texts that cover such issues, and one might argue it is worse to initiate these discussions badly than not doing it at all. Does a teacher who is asked to cover suicide, whether in Shakespeare's *Romeo and Juliet* or John Green's *Looking for Alaska*, feel comfortable initiating these conversations? Are they confident they know what to do if a student makes a concerning comment or disclosure? Do they feel the school leadership would support them if they didn't get something quite right, or a parent raised an issue? We argue that, whilst the potential of this kind of study is enormous, the answer to all of these questions needs to be 'yes' before it can be successful (see Duncan-Andrade and Morrell 2008). Debates around teacher-led and student-led discussion are often centred on the assumption that one or other is preferred based on whose voice and contribution is deemed to have the most value. We argue that it is vitally important to think about this through the lens of teacher confidence too: it is a perfectly reasonable act of self-preservation to want to avoid opportunities for student talk if you are scared of what they might say. It is understandable that a teacher may want to position themselves as the expert if their actual conviction in this sentiment is insecure, especially if they fear a more open (and thus unpredictable) pedagogic approach might reveal them as an imposter. This is a fundamental issue around training and support, and not something individual teachers should be vilified for.

Equally there may be pragmatic limitations that arise from what else has been covered already further down the school or is planned to be covered further up. Some texts may require parental consent to study them with a class, meaning some books may not be considered if even a few parents refuse permission. These constraints are real and need to be acknowledged. Working in concert with these practical considerations, however, are the ideological and philosophical beliefs of the school, department and individual teacher, regarding what the perceived 'point' of the unit, and studying fiction per se, should be.

4.3 Schema theory

One productive way in which it is possible to think through the advantages and disadvantages of different text choices is to draw on schema theory, introduced in Chapter 1 (Section 1.2), and in particular the concept of narrative schemas.

The notion of schemas crops up in various academic disciplines and has been discussed in relation to the psychology of reading literature since as early as the 1930s (Bartlett 1932). Schema theory makes simple claims about how our background knowledge is organised in the mind, and how we retrieve relevant information as and when we need it, without having to wade through other elements of our knowledge which are of no use to us in a given moment. In other words, schema theory is a simple foundational idea within cognitive linguistics, which offers a more systematic way of thinking about and describing the interactions between prior knowledge and our day-to-day interactions in and with the world. In schema theory, 'relevant associated chunks of our knowledge are formed into schemas, which we access in order to make sense of the new situations on a daily basis' (Giovanelli and Mason 2018a: 71). Schemas help us to understand and navigate current experiences, whether that involves walking down the street or reading a Shakespeare play.

Schema theory characterises the knowledge we all carry around in our minds as incremental, interrelated, and something which builds and develops over time. For instance, prior to March 2020 most people upon hearing the words 'pandemic' or 'lockdown' would have had limited schematic knowledge to draw on, and younger children in particular may have had no sense of what these words meant at all. Most people would have 'accreted' (meaning accrued or gained) their knowledge of these two concepts at an attenuated distance, perhaps from reading about them, seeing them in films or hearing about rare instances of them on the news. A few people, such as virologists and dystopian fiction fans and writers, however, will have had rich and diverse schematic knowledge of one or both of these concepts. Even for these people, though, this knowledge will have likely been theoretical, fictional or academic. Writing this in lockdown as the direct result of a global pandemic, the situation now is very different. Now, experiential and rapid schema accretion for these two concepts has been almost universal. At the same time, our schemas for 'lockdown' and 'pandemic' will likely have some broad similarities but also contain nuanced variations depending on our country, region, personal circumstance and so on. The same is true of our knowledge of all words, concepts, ideas, events and actions: this is the basic claim of schema theory.

Stockwell (2020: 106–107) operationalises this theory as a cognitive poetic framework, offering a useful set of metalinguistic terms to enable systematised discussion of how new and existing knowledge interacts:

- Tuning – the modifications of facts or relations within the schema.
- Restructuring – the creation of new schemas.
- Schema reinforcement – where incoming facts on you but strengthen unconfirmed schematic knowledge.
- Schema accretion – where new facts are added to an existing schema, enlarging its scope and explanatory range.

Mason (2019: 66) goes on to elaborate four key points about this cognitive linguistic model:

1. The mind is able to call up not just individual items of knowledge, but also coherent chunks of related information (that is, a schema), which is one reason schema theory is especially useful as a descriptive tool.
2. Humans can enjoy virtually immediate mental access to their knowledge schemas and tune generic versions to highly individualised ones at will, and without confusion or effort.
3. Schemas can be accreted by any information the individual perceives is related, even emotional responses such as fear, and accretion and tuning does not need to be the result of direct experience.
4. Schemas are unique to individuals are likely to have high degrees of overlap with others, especially those who share culture, background, experiences, and so on.

Importantly, our schemas are not fixed and stable, but instead are transient and dynamic. So, when needed, our mind rapidly calls up and 'soft-assembles' a schema containing the prior knowledge it perceives will help us make sense of the current context. Stockwell (2020: 176) explains:

> We need to keep in mind the fact that concepts (such as objects, places, and people) are soft assembled for the situation in hand. In other words, every configuration of properties, experiences, relations, and associations that cloud around a particular concept is brought together afresh on every occasion of use.

The fact that our prior knowledge isn't stable is often overlooked in passing references to schemas in education discourse. As such, when a student or a teacher enters the classroom, they bring with them an individualised mental bank of potential resources and tools. This background knowledge will necessarily inform the interactions they then have with the space, texts, information, and other people in that school and in that classroom. This might take the form of a positive or negative attitude towards the subject based on that individual's prior experiences ('I like English'; 'I hate physics'), a sense of whether something will be easy or hard ('I'm good at reading'; 'I'm bad at algebra'), enjoyable or dull. These schemas are subject to change: a bad mark might form a central part of a student's schema for a subject one week, enjoyment of the text being currently studied the next. A person's available schematic knowledge and the schemas they go on to assemble from this potential pool of resources is also very likely to inform comprehension and accessibility of new information. This makes schema theory a useful and productive lens through which to think about all educational activities and, as we now demonstrate, offers particularly salient ways of thinking about the study of fiction.

4.4 Narrative schemas

As discussed in the previous chapter, the literature classroom is a specific discourse environment in which participants (teacher and students) are largely 'unequal' (Fairclough 2014) in status, where roles and routines are essentially mapped out (Edwards and Westgate 1994), and where ground rules for educational practice are established and adhered to (Edwards and Mercer 2013). The teacher remains an authority figure, able to influence how reading is enacted and the types of interpretation that are legitimised and positioned as preferred responses to literary texts. In the majority of circumstances where teachers introduce texts to their classes, there is also an imbalance of knowledge and experience; generally, teachers are re-readers guiding students who are first-time readers (we discussed the distinctions between first time and re-reading extensively in Chapter 3; see in particular Section 3.1).

It is therefore possible to apply schema theory to reading in a group, including the school classroom, using the idea of 'narrative schemas' (Mason 2014, 2016, 2019; Giovanelli and Mason 2015). A teacher reading a set text with a group, along with every student in the room, will have a unique narrative schema for the text. This narrative schema is each person's available mental version of the novel, which is the resource they will draw on as they read, think about, talk about or write about it. When planning tasks or discussing the text with students, therefore, it's useful to bear in mind that as a re-reader of the text, teachers will typically have:

- much more richly accreted narrative schemas than their students
- narrative schemas containing accreted elements from points in the text that the students have not yet reached

As the class progresses through the novel, each person will accrete their narrative schema, not only from their own reading, but also from any other knowledge about the text they encounter. Crucially this can include what a teacher (or peer) *says* about the text.

As a person reads, they 'tune' incoming elements of the story against the information they have already accreted in their narrative schema. This is why readers don't like spoilers and tend to avoid engaging in conversations with people who have read more of a text than they have. If another reader tells you a plot point you have not yet read about for yourself, you accrete that information before you were supposed to, and then cannot help but tune the remainder of your reading in light of that knowledge. In other words, premature accretion disrupts personal response (Giovanelli and Mason 2015). This is the key distinction between reading a text for the first time and re-reading it thereafter: as a first-time reader you accrete your narrative schema as you go, any reading thereafter is tuned against your existing narrative schema. This is the distinction we feel when we re-read or re-watch a story knowing the plot twist or reveal at the end. Often, we will begin to notice hints and clues that we were oblivious to the first time we encountered it, or a twist may even come to seem obvious. This is because, now being able to mentally assemble a narrative schema containing the full story arc and its details, all subsequent encounters are tuned against this knowledge.

The classroom, then, is a reading environment where students without rich narrative schemas for a text are led through it by a teacher with a highly accreted narrative schema at their disposal. There is then the potential for lesson tasks and teacher discourse to interfere with students' authentic engagement with the text. This can manifest itself in teachers deciding which elements of a lesson's reading is going to form the basis of the task(s), which learning objectives are going to be addressed and how meeting them is going to be achieved. The teacher, being mindful of what the tasks are, targets the lesson around these points. If this focus is relayed to the students before the reading takes place, then it can effectively narrow the scope of study and thereby privilege and legitimise only those responses to a text that coincide with the pre-stated aims. In these cases, we argue that the teacher is pre-figuring the students' attention (discussed further in Chapter 5). In such lessons, what is relevant to the lesson tasks and objectives forms the focus; other potential avenues of interest are likely to be backgrounded, along with anything students may have wanted to discuss or explore further which does not cohere with the predetermined lesson plan (Turvey and Lloyd 2014). In these instances, opportunities to capitalise on and interrelate students' reading with the knowledge and experience they bring to the classroom – not only authentic but critically useful student engagement with the text – are unnecessarily grounded because they do not cohere with a pre-planned emphasis.

Narrative schemas thus help us to describe more precisely the challenge that English teachers face on a daily basis: how to manage one's own rich narrative schema whilst also guiding students to accrete their own, without imposing interpretations and therefore manufacturing their readings, or revealing forthcoming text knowledge which will ultimately tune students' narrative schemas away from their own reading of the text towards learning the teacher's instead.

4.4.1 Narrative schemas, comprehension and 'challenge'

Discussions around appropriate text choices in literary study often rightly orient to debates around challenge. We posit, however, that examining this debate using the concept of narrative schemas highlights that it can be problematic to restrict consideration of challenge solely to questions of how easy or difficult the language, structure or plot of a text is to comprehend. Required levels of literacy is one important aspect, but only one aspect, of factors that determine whether or not a course in studying fiction will be 'challenging'.

A simple conflation of the level of 'challenge' a text choice represents in terms of literacy and comprehension requirements on the one hand, with the level of academic rigour a unit on that text will therefore involve on the other is, from a cognitive point of view, a misnomer. This is because, as we described in Chapter 3, knowledge a person accretes about any text can come from two sources:

1. The direct act of reading the text.
2. Discourse encountered about the text (such as what a teacher or peers say about it; reviews, critical material or summaries read or watched; the blurb on the back, and so on).

For every text a person comes across, whether they read it or not, they accrete a narrative schema for that text, which might span from skeletal to rich and highly populated. This then forms the potential knowledge they have available for a later act of soft-assembly. This does not mean that all this information will remain available to them, as it may 'decay' from memory over time and cease to be accessible, or the other contextual cues that prompts reassembly of that narrative schema might work to background some aspects that are not perceived as relevant. This is how people can manage to talk confidently about books they've never opened. Indeed, the *Talking About Texts* study discussed in Chapter 3 found that 38.6% of respondents said that they may lie about reading a book they hadn't read, in certain circumstances. The only reason we are able to do this is because a narrative schema can be accreted to our mental archive of texts without the need to actually read it.

Highly rigorous and academic units can be designed using texts which present a lower level of challenge from a comprehension point of view: this is intuitively obvious when we reflect on the volume of university modules at both undergraduate and postgraduate level, as well as the amount of academic scholarship which focuses on popular culture texts, Young Adult and Children's fiction, films and music lyrics, to name but a few.

Equally, units based on canonical or very dense and difficult texts, with significant literacy barriers which must be overcome for students to successfully access the content, can be reductive and lack challenge. This can happen when students are so necessarily reliant on their teacher's discourse about the text in order to make sense of it that their narrative schema is predominantly accreted by that discourse, and not their own interaction and engagement with the text itself. The interpretations and responses they are then able to produce will almost certainly be heavily manufactured because very little authentic reading will have populated their narrative schema in the first place. We argue that there can thus be a danger in exclusively selecting texts which require high levels of skill in terms of literacy for students to comprehend for themselves; specifically, that students can end up accreting their narrative schemas for these texts from their teacher's discourse about the text rather than from the direct act of reading. This is, crucially, not to denigrate either pole of text choice in principle, but merely to suggest that scrutinising the design and content of a unit is perhaps a better way to assess its challenge rather than basing this evaluation solely on the text.

What particularly problematises this debate is that choosing between canonical or classic literature on the one hand and popular culture or Young Adult fiction on the other is that so often framed as a binary either/or decision. Worse, this is then often mapped onto other binaries: a choice of academic rigour versus pandering to student interest; knowledge or relevance; cultural literacy or dumbing-down the curriculum. This is highly frustrating and something we ourselves have fallen foul of in a piece we published in the *TES* (*Times Educational Supplement*) (Giovanelli and Mason 2016). Discussing the fact that students bring a wealth of schematic knowledge about texts they choose to engage with (in any medium: books they read for pleasure, films and television programmes they watch, the music they listen to, the life experiences they have), here is what we actually said in the article:

> Students' schematic knowledge is often downplayed, and their reading of non-canonical texts in particular maligned. For example, young adult fiction regularly receives heavy criticism from some quarters. Teachers who do choose to engage this knowledge can be variously accused of dumbing-down, lowering expectations or pandering to students' interests when they should be (inferentially and sometimes explicitly) be teaching them about Shakespeare, Donne or Chaucer.
> This fundamentally misrepresents the position adopted by most advocates for acknowledging student expertise who, by and large, suggest an integrated approach that involves the accrual of knowledge and "cultural capital", and attending to the wealth of knowledge that students bring to the classroom with them: the two are by no means mutually exclusive [...] this is also utterly contrary to what we know about reading and cognition.
> (Giovanelli and Mason 2016: 34)

The *TES* then chose to publish the article under the title 'Why You Should Ditch the Canon', framing even this argument against viewing text choices as a binary ... as a binary. Until we can overcome this pervasive tendency to present the discussion of text choice as a polarised 'either/or' we will never make significant progress.

Duncan-Andrade (2007, 2010a) has undertaken some highly successful and ground-breaking research in this area, as both a practitioner and an academic. He explains the importance of unpicking this false binary using as his example the work of Tupac Shakur – an iconic and influential figure for his own students – in Oakland, California. He argues, 'you are not socially just if you are not giving kids an academically rigorous curriculum' but, at the same time, he champions the importance of also taking texts and authors young people enjoy and choose to engage with seriously:

> feel how you want about Tupac, I'm critical of him as well [...] But what I know for a *fact* is that from my youth to the youth I work with today, 'Pac has been incredibly influential and as educators it is our *job* to understand: what are the things that are influencing our young people's world view? To understand those in a profound way rather than to continue to dismiss youth culture as a phase
> (Duncan-Andrade 2010b).

Activities and Reflections

1. What is your initial response to Duncan-Andrade's viewpoint? Do you agree? Why? Why not?
2. If understanding youth culture and young people's world view is part of being an educator, do you feel appropriately supported in developing your knowledge and understanding in these areas? What might good teacher CPD in this area look like?
3. One concern that is sometimes levied at an argument like Duncan-Andrade's is that educators will come across as insincere or else appear to be aligning themselves unnecessarily with youth culture. Do you think there is legitimacy to these concerns? If so, are they possible to successfully navigate? How?

One view of education that is particularly critical of the study of texts from genres such as Young Adult and Children's literature is the cultural literacy model (Hirsch et al. 1988; Hirsch 2007). Looked at from this perspective, there is less value in even the most challenging and rigorous units that focus on or include popular culture texts, Young Adult texts or films when compared to those focusing on the classics and canonical works. This is because the cultural literacy model uses the perceived level of cultural capital associated with a text choice as a key metric of its value. Whilst we would by no means dismiss potential gains in cultural capital as one of many relevant considerations when selecting a diet of texts a student will encounter over the course of their school career, it is also important to incorporate reflection on some of the problematic underpinnings of this line of argument.

First, as discussed in Chapter 2, it is worth bearing in mind that Hirsch explicitly advocates for manufactured reading practices, arguing that what is of most importance is that young people know *about* particular texts, and not that they actually read them. We feel that whatever your views of cultural literacy are, it is worth reflecting on whether this aligns with the aims you are trying to achieve when studying fiction with young people. Authentic skills of critical interpretation require personal engagement with texts, not simply learning about them. Second, cultural literacy is heavily founded on a deficit (rather than difference) model of knowledge: one of his key works on this approach is in fact called *The Knowledge Deficit* (2007). These approaches have been strongly critiqued for the ways in which they overlook and delegitimise knowledge that is not held up by white, middle class, formally educated Western traditions, and as a result positions students with different backgrounds as lacking (for an excellent critique of deficit models in education see Jones 2013). As Jones (2013) discusses, Bernstein's notion of 'restricted' and 'elaborated' codes (Bernstein 1964) is problematic for the same reason. This second critique is particularly relevant when considering the construction of socially just inclusive curricula. Steele (2010) explains, from the perspective of social psychology, that there can be profound negative effects of even tacit communication to students that characteristics they possess (such as race, class or ethnicity) are associated with their likelihood of doing well or otherwise: pervasive stereotypes can impact actual academic performance. In other words, if a curriculum is founded on the principles of a deficit model then any hint of this that is outwardly apparent can further disadvantage the very students such approaches are aiming to help: being aware that you are less likely to succeed in a topic or assessment actually makes you less likely to do so.

4.5 Text choice and equitable education

The penultimate section of this chapter builds on these discussions about the relative potential benefits and limitations of different text choices for different students and considers questions of equity and inclusivity in literature education.

4.5.1 Inclusivity and the literature classroom

The discourse surrounding text choices has always incorporated discussions around inclusivity and enfranchisement, with a particular recognition that selecting different texts as the focus of study will, as an inevitable by-product, advantage some students and disadvantage others. This might be, for example, through alignments with individual background knowledge, preferences or interests, a result of the people, places and events represented in the text, or even the degree of familiarity with the broader cultural tradition in which the text is situated.

However, Duncan-Andrade and Morrell (2008) caution against simply incorporating 'diverse' texts or authors within the literature curriculum as an effective resolution to the risk of systematically advantaging white middle class children, arguing for a change in the way we approach texts, rather than necessarily the texts themselves. They argue:

> we firmly believed that literacy educators could encourage a multicultural reading of any text [...] we were wary of those educators and literary theorists who equated multiculturalism with simply offering texts written by people of colour or focusing on people of colour as protagonists. As students and educators, we witnessed practices around these so-called multicultural texts that were equally, if not more, disempowering of students of colour than more traditional and less diverse texts. An oppressive rendering of a culturally diverse text is still oppressive
>
> (Duncan-Andrade and Morrell 2008: 52).

This is a powerful point that is often overlooked in discussions around text choice and the study of fiction, and it extends well beyond multicultural inclusivity, though this of course is a vital consideration for all schools. That is, it is easy to adopt the passive assumption that text choice dictates course focus, when in fact this is far from the truth. It *is* true of course that most units on George Orwell's *Animal Farm* will tend to give a central role to its allegorical connections to the Russian revolution, but this is because teachers and schools are *choosing* to do so, even if that choice is largely only because of the overwhelming primacy typically given to that particular reading of the text. It seems uncontroversial to suggest that proposing a unit of study that decentralised or even removed discussion of Russian history would require a degree of bravery. Nonetheless, the text itself offers, whilst not limitless, myriad other possibilities for alternative focuses, many of which could achieve an aim of inclusive curriculum. For instance, it is easy to see how the prototypical discussion of class could be amended and extended to a discussion of race. The representations of gender in the novella could offer an equally academically rigorous unit. In other words, it is perfectly possible to craft an inclusive unit around a traditional text.

It is possible too, to examine the absences in a text and reconsider it through hypothetical alternatives. In his seminal work *Textual Intervention* (1995) Rob Pope explores, for example, the power of rewriting, reimagining or otherwise intervening in a text as a mechanism to better understand its component parts and the role they play in meaning making and interpretation. In this way, units need not be limited to analysing what is present in the text, but also what is missing. How might Golding's *Lord of the Flies* have been different if the crashed plane had been full of girls, not boys, for instance? If Dr Jekyll/Mr Hyde had taken place in 2020 what would this change? What if Robert Louis Stephenson had explicitly framed the character as having a mental health diagnosis? What if Romeo was a woman or Juliet male, or what if one of them was transgender? What if the play had been set in South Africa in the era of apartheid? What if Kathy and Heathcliff were of Asian heritage? What if Jane Eyre had cerebral palsy? Textual interventions can be a fruitful way of diversifying and making more inclusive texts when the economic constraints discussed in Section 4.3 dictate the text choice itself (see this chapter's Further Reading).

> **Activities and Reflections**
>
> Choose one of the texts you currently teach.
> 1. Imagine you had to redesign it without any of the current themes you focus on. What would you cover instead?
> 2. Imagine you had to redesign it as a more inclusive course. What would you do with it?
> 3. What are your anxieties about discussing issues like sexism, racism, LGBTQ+ rights and ableism in the classroom? What would it take for you to feel confident and comfortable navigating a unit that focused on one or more of these topics?

Discussions around inclusivity and the literature curriculum often circle back to the question of what 'English' and the study of fiction is 'for'. Concerns are sometimes raised about whether in making literary study more diverse and inclusive, especially if this is enacted through text choice, academic rigor is being sacrificed for pastoral care or political correctness. To this we would simply offer that all text choices and unit designs necessarily advantage and enfranchise some students already. If that group is consistently the same one, then it is hard to see that others are not being structurally and systematically disenfranchised as a result.

4.6 Paracanons

We end this chapter with brief discussion of Stimpson's notion of a 'paracanon' as an alternative way of thinking about what we value in terms of text choices. She writes

> Texts are paracanonical if some people have loved and do love them [...] No matter how difficult or accessible, how 'high' or 'low', any text is eligible for inclusion in a paracanon if it is beloved [...] The notion of a paracanon can be a pedagogical tool, a way of organising the classroom and a syllabus. Using it, a teacher can foreground the experiences of reading that teacher and students actually have. The teacher can then assist the class in placing these experiences within larger cultural patterns. Why was *this* text loved? By whom? Was *this* text not loved, but hated, love's demonic other? Why? By whom? And did *this* text find only indifference? Did it look for love in the wrong places?
>
> (Stimpson 1990: 972)

We shall return to the issue of canonical writers and the curriculum in Chapter 7. At this point, and in the context of our discussion in this chapter, we would suggest that the concept of paracanon (a body of texts that readers have said they have enjoyed and which have made lasting impressions of readers unrelated to any *canonical* status they might or might not have acquired) offers a powerful way for teachers to think about the kinds of texts that could – and should – be read in classrooms. We would also suggest that drawing on paracanonical texts in the classroom offers an opportunity for teachers and students to engage in thinking about some of the issues surrounding text choices themselves and to critically consider ideas of value and worth in relation to curriculum time. In our view, the paracanon raises important questions about the very purpose of studying fiction in schools and the significance of the emotional aspect of reading in relation to school English. We shall return to this question in Chapter 8.

Further reading

Quigley (2020) offers an excellent consideration of text choices in relation to developing literacy and comprehension skills, as well as student confidence. For a comprehensive exploration of socially just education in English see Duncan-Andrade and Morrell (2008). Duncan-Andrade's (2010b) Harvard lecture is also excellent on this topic and includes extensive discussion of debates surrounding text choices and popular culture. Alternatively, the lecture is based on Duncan-Andrade (2009), an article published in the *Harvard Educational Review*. Duncan-Andrade and Morrell (2008) outline academically rigorous units combining canonical and popular texts that have been implemented and successfully used by teachers.

Hopper (2006) offers a detailed account of why teachers might find it hard to know which texts to choose in a context where Young Adult and Children's literature has been downplayed on assessment specifications. Turvey and Lloyd (2014) critically reflects on time pressures and the ways concerns about opportunity cost can manifest in the literature classroom. Pope (1995) offers a host of excellent ideas about, and a comprehensive practical guide to, undertaking textual intervention exercises with students as suggested in Section 4. Another practically oriented text we would highly recommend is Scott (2014), which explores using frameworks and methods from across stylistics to teach creative writing to students.

5
ATTENTION

This chapter will:

- introduce key research on the psychology of attention, in particular the concepts of 'figure-ground' and 'burying';
- explore the role of attention in different types of reading;
- introduce the concepts of 'immersion' and 'transportation' and explore its connections with attention;
- introduce the notion of 'pre-figuring';
- look at ways in which texts can manipulate readers' attention and offer examples of ways in which figure-ground can be used as a tool of analysis.

5.1 Understanding attention

Attention is a zero-sum game. What this means is we all have a finite amount of capacity to pay attention to things; we cannot exponentially increase our ability to focus on as many things as we like. As a result, focusing on one thing always comes at the cost of drawing our attention away from something else. When we think of ourselves as 'multitasking' what we are actually doing is switching our attention very rapidly from one task to another, sometimes called 'toggling'. Many activities inherently require us to toggle our attention. A classic example of this is driving, where at any time we might be toggling our attention between looking straight ahead, looking in mirrors, changing gears, keeping an eye on speed, looking at other vehicles in the immediate vicinity, looking at potential traffic and hazards further away, checking road signs, talking to other people in the car and so on. Experienced and competent drivers are often able to manage these different demands on their attention so easily that they have little or no conscious awareness of doing it; they can experience 'flow' (Csikszentmihalyi 1996, 2014) or 'immersion' in their driving such that time can pass without their notice, or they may get out of the car with little memory of the journey. This is the same phenomenon commonly reported amongst avid gamers and readers, and will be discussed more extensively below (see Section 5.7.2). Crucially, however, this does not mean that attention, even for seasoned drivers, is limitless (though high levels of confidence can give people this impression of their own capacity). This is why it is so dangerous to check a phone or text whilst driving: it is impossible to do this without compensating by reducing attention on being in control of the vehicle.

Cognitive psychology terms this shifting of our attention as figure-ground configuration. For example, the image below is conceptualised as either four white squares on a black background or as a black cross against a white background. It is impossible to see both at the same time (although you can toggle quickly between them). This is because at any time one must be prominent in our attention and form Figure 5.1, with the other necessarily remaining as the ground.

FIGURE 5.1 Figure and Ground

5.2 Attention and reading

Figure-ground configuration is a natural cognitive phenomenon; it is something we cannot help but do. Without figure-ground, our visual, aural and kinaesthetic capacities[1] would collapse. Everything would be an overwhelming and indistinguishable assault of colours, shapes, sounds and sensations. Simply put, because we cannot pay attention to everything at once, we constantly select from moment to moment what to pay attention to and what to ignore. This can be done consciously and deliberately but mostly happens below the level of our conscious awareness. This is an innate and fundamental part of successfully navigating through the world, of keeping ourselves safe in the face of the numerous inputs we are receiving from our environment at any given moment, even right now as you read this. Because of this, psychologists have discovered that there is often a sound evolutionary logic underpinning the things that make good attractors of our attention (Evans and Green 2006; Haber and Hershenson 1980; Ungerer and Schmid 2013). The beast running towards us or the snake slithering on the floor merits more attention than the tree. The hand on your shoulder demands notice more than the sensation of grass underfoot. The sound of running water is more advantageous to hear than the whistling of the wind. That is, most of our attention is dictated by what our brain thinks will keep us safe. At the same time, we could choose to reorient our focus to the tree, the grass, the sounds of the wind if we wanted to: we have natural pulls acting on our attentional system, but we can also exert our agency and control over it.

A fundamental principle of cognitive linguistics is that the ways in which we process and engage with texts mirrors the ways we process and engage with everything else. As such, close examination of figure-ground configurations in, for example, a literary work, can uncover the ways in which it positions a reader or listener's attention; how it naturally pulls about and plays with our mind's eye. Much of the practice of textual analysis involves enacting our powers of control over this focus, to look in detail at the text's component parts.

In cognitive poetics, researchers, most notably Stockwell (2009), have applied this knowledge from psychology to examine the role of figure-ground in reading literature. It is important in order to engage in this kind of analysis to understand what informs the moment to moment, largely subconscious, decisions about what to figure and what to leave in the ground. To this end, Stockwell offers a list of features of good attentional attractors:

- **Newness** (new objects, characters, scenes, movements: the present moment of reading is more attractive than the previous moment)
- **Agency** (noun phrases in the active position are better attractors than in the passive position)
- **Topicality** (noun phrases in the subject position are more likely to be figures than those in the object position)
- **Empathetic recognisability** (human speaker > human hearer > animal > object > abstraction)
- **Definiteness** (definite ('the man') > a specific indefinite ('a certain man') > non-specific indefinite ('any man'))
- **Activeness** (verbs denoting action, violence, passion, wilfulness, motivation or strength)
- **Brightness** (lightness or vivid colours attract attention over dimness or drabness)
- **Fullness** (richness, density, intensity or nutrition)
- **Largeness** (large objects)
- **Height** (objects that are above others, are higher than the perceiver, or which dominate the scene)
- **Noisiness** (anything which makes sound or is noisy relative to other things in the scene)
- **Aesthetic distance from the norm** (beautiful or ugly referents, dangerous referents, alien objects denoted, unusual things)

(adapted from Stockwell 2009: 31).

Stockwell's model of attentional attractors operationalises the phenomenon of figure-ground as a cognitive poetic framework, supplying a list of features able to be identified within texts. He advocates using this framework as a productive and robust means of tracking patterns of foregrounded and backgrounded elements within written texts. We echo that claim, and here extend it to encourage consideration of studying fiction: not just the attentional pulls in the text but also in the classroom.

5.3 Attention and text analysis

We will now demonstrate how figure-ground can be utilised as a tool for textual analysis. For example, in an extract from page 234 of *Harry Potter and the Chamber of Secrets*, J. K. Rowling's second book in the *Harry Potter* series. In this scene, the reader's attention. is repeatedly toggled between Harry and a giant serpent – a Basilisk – which is first in the process of being summoned, and then emerges from a large dark hole. First, our attention is drawn to the hole itself, which is achieved predominantly by utilising the attentional attractors of activeness and largeness: Slytherin's mouth is first noted as 'moving' and then expanding 'opening wider and wider, to make a huge black hole'. Even though the snake is not at first very definite – being originally referred to as 'something' – it is repeatedly given agency and topicality by being placed in the subject position in active sentence constructions. It then becomes more definite through very particular verbs being used to describe its motion: 'slithering' is rarely used to refer to the movements of anything other than a snake. Finally, this pull to figure the snake is compounded through an additional reference to its hugeness and also noisiness, as readers, we hear it 'hit' the stone floor of the chamber. Interestingly, as is often the case in fictional texts, the protagonist's attention mirrors and therefore reinforces the direction of our own: the newness, activeness, hugeness and noisiness of the serpent attracts Harry's attention, just as it attracts ours.

> **Activities and Reflections**
>
> 1. Select an extract from a text or poem that you teach or have taught and try out this kind of figure-ground analysis. You could do this with your students, perhaps starting with Stockwell's list of attractors (which you could abridge for ease: movement, newness, brightness and noisiness are probably the most accessible) and asking them to try to spot any of these characteristics. How useful or illuminating did you find this approach?
> 2. Ask students to rewrite a section of text to change the figure-ground configuration. You could perhaps ask them to background a figured character and give prominence to another, or figure an element of the setting. Then reflect together on how this changes the text. Rewriting exercises are always a good way to help understand how stylistic choices and features within a text work.

5.4 Thematic figure-ground

At a thematic level, we can use figure-ground to explain broad interpretations of whole texts. For example, readers of Mary Shelley's *Frankenstein*, might feel sympathy and admiration for Victor, or see him as an over-reacher and unattractive in contrast, perhaps, to the Creature. In this instance, one interpretation necessarily becomes the figure and pushes the other into the ground; both readings are of course possible, but it is not possible to see both at the same time (although, again, it is possible to toggle relatively quickly between them). Considering multiple possible interpretations or shifting wholesale thematic focus is thus a great mental exercise in essentially reconfiguring the text; pulling a chained set of figures to the fore of attention and thus, necessarily, leaving other things in the ground. This is fundamentally what most theme-based exam questions ask students to do, making this ability vital for success as an English specialist (whether as a teacher or a student), at least in terms of assessment. That is, students are asked in examinations to rapidly reconfigure their perspective on a text figuring a theme they may well have been asked to consider for the first time upon opening the paper. Assessment, then, frames this as a central skill for mastery in studying fiction.

Activities and Reflections

1. Choose a text and consider one of the following themes within it – love, power, betrayal, death, wisdom or honour (or another of your choosing). Which aspects of the text are pulled into the figure of your attention? What is left in the ground? How does this frame your response to the text in this particular configuration?
2. Take the same text from Question 1. Select and reflect on a different theme. Reflect on how this reconfigures your attention on different elements. Does it change your response to the text? Do you like it more or less? Do you find it more or less interesting or engaging?
3. Try these exercises in actively reconfiguring attention on different themes with your students. Reflect with them on how focusing on different elements can change the feel of the text and their responses to it.

5.5 Burying

Psychological research shows that 'figured' elements of a text are subject to greater depth of processing (Sanford 2002; Sanford and Sturt 2002; Sanford and Emmott 2012), and can be attributed "narrative world salience"; we tend to assume they are important (Emmott and Alexander 2014). However, just as things can pull and attract our attention, so too can we be manipulated to miss things. Considering how and why we *don't* pay attention to things is just as important as understanding when we do. This phenomenon in texts is undertaken through a strategy called 'burying'. Emmott and Alexander (2014: 329) explain:

> placing information in the background is not usually viewed as a major strategic choice. Nevertheless, for plot purposes, deliberately burying information in the background of a text is highly strategic. By "burying" we mean that information is placed in the background with the intention that it should not be easily found

Emmott and Alexander explore how burying is enacted in literary texts, especially crime fiction, where it is often fundamental that readers and viewers are supplied with the right information to potentially be able to work out 'whodunnit', but ideally either do not notice or do not recognise the salience of these features the first time round. As Stockwell (2009) did for figure-ground, Emmott and Alexander (2014) compile a comprehensive list of strategies used to 'bury' information within a text:

1. Mention the item as little as possible.
2. Use linguistic structures which have been shown to reduce prominence, such as embedding within a subordinate clause.
3. Under-specify the item, describing it in a way that is sufficiently imprecise that it draws little attention to it or detracts from features that are relevant to the plot.
4. Place the item next to an item that is more prominent, so that the focus is on the latter.

5. Make the item apparently unimportant in the narrative world (even though it is actually significant).
6. Make it difficult for the reader to make inferences by splitting up information needed to do so.
7. Place information in positions where a reader is distracted or not yet interested.
8. Stress one specific aspect of the item so that another aspect becomes less prominent.
9. Give the item a false significance, so that the real significance is buried.
10. Get the narrator or characters in the story to say that the item is uninteresting.
11. Discredit the characters reporting certain information, making both seem less credible or important.

(adapted from Emmott and Alexander 2014: 332)

Figuring and burying techniques often work in concert: pulling attention towards one thing and in doing so distracting from another. So too in education contexts we are often not only directing students' attention towards certain things but burying others in the process. This will now be explored in more detail.

5.6 Burying and reading

The latter part of this chapter is going to consider how these complementary concepts – figure-ground and burying – can be fruitfully employed in classroom and lesson design. However, before applying these ideas more broadly let's consider how close analysis of figure-ground and burying can illuminate the mechanics of a literary work. This, we argue, is an accessible and highly productive approach to any text that can offer students a valuable tool to support their analysis. In particular, this style of analysis works well for texts where there is a reveal or twist.

The extract below is taken from the short story 'The Man Who Loved Flowers' by Stephen King, taken from his 1978 collection *Night Shift*. Through the unfortunate necessity of demonstrating this kind of approach, however, we are about to reveal a spoiler relating to the story and would therefore implore anyone wishing to retain an authentic first-time reading to pause here and go and read it first. It is only 16 pages.

> The young man crossed Sixty-third street, walking with a bounce in his step and that same half-smile on his lips. Part way up the block, an old man stood beside a chipped green handcart filled with flowers – the predominant colour was yellow; a yellow fever of jonquils and late crocuses. The old man also had carnations and a few hothouse tea roses, mostly yellow and white.
>
> [...]
>
> The radio poured out bad news that no one listened to: a hammer murderer was still on the loose; JFK had declared that the situation in a little Asian country called Vietnam ('Vite-num' the guy reading the news called it) would bear watching; an unidentified woman had been pulled from the East River; a grand jury had failed to indict a crime overlord in the current city administration's war on heroin; the Russians had exploded a nuclear device.
>
> (King 1978: 291–2)

Later, the young man passes the flower stall and decides that he will buy some flowers for 'her' (we assume a girlfriend or wife).

54 Attention

First consider the ebbs and flows of figuring that moves the reader through this passage and story. At a macro-level analysis, the easiest way to begin is to generate a simple summary of what happens. Here, it would be something like: 'an unknown young man walks down a street, passing a flower cart with some sounds coming from a radio, then he stops and turns back to buy some flowers from the cart'. This kind of summarising exercise will typically reveal what was most prominently figured as these become the things we include. Our summary here suggests the young man, the cart, the radio and then perhaps the flowers are all figured at some point. Closer examination supports this.

The first paragraph gives 'the young man' topicality and agency (he is in the subject position in an active construction), activeness (he moves), empathetic recognisability (he is human) and a relative degree of definiteness (he is 'the' young man, not 'a' young man). This definiteness and recognisability is increased as the reader zooms in on specific features: his bouncing step (activeness) and his 'half-smile'. Most of these qualities are repeatedly attributed to the young man throughout the passage, notably when focus returns to him in paragraphs three and four.

Following the young man's introduction, figuring is temporarily diverted to a new character who quickly escalates in his degree of definiteness (from 'an' old man to 'the' old man) and his cart. Following the principle of empathetic recognisability, the man should act as a better attentional attractor than the cart, however, the cart arguably pulls more focus and it is interesting to unpick how this is achieved. Whilst the old man is repeatedly positioned as the subject in sentences and attributed several verb processes as an active participant (topicality and agency), on closer inspection, none of his actions involve much or any movement. The cart and its flowers by contrast are imbued with several attentional attractors, most notably newness and brightness. Three different colours are attributed to the cart and flowers, most notably 'yellow' which is made more prominent through repetition. Four specific types of flowers are named, giving them a strong degree of definiteness. In other words, the passage stacks the deck in favour of the cart and the flowers when by rights the old man should probably be most likely to attract the reader's focus. The second paragraph ends by attributing largeness and newness to a description of a bulky transistor radio' but intriguingly not definiteness, topicality, agency or, yet, noisiness: the reader is encouraged to figure it in their attention, but not strongly.

This anticipated noisiness appears at the opening of the next paragraph as the radio 'pours out' sound in the form of 'bad news'. Interestingly again though this attractor is somewhat muted as we are told that none of the characters are actually listening to it. Nonetheless the reader is then zoomed into the world of the radio and tracked through a series of stories with an arguably escalating degree of seriousness.

Interestingly, as the story progresses, we are encouraged to shift the radio fully back into the ground as we are told that its sound fades, we realise we have continued to track the path of the young man the whole time: the radio has become noisy and figured for us as he passes the cart and it would become noisy and figured for him, and as he moves further away this attractor fades for both of us and we turn our attention to other things. His attention somewhat freed up by the fading of the radio, it would seem, we finally follow the young man pausing and then turning his attention back to the cart, this time figuring not the radio, but the flowers, which he decides to buy.

This figure-ground analysis tracks a first-time reading of this story, offering a fairly comprehensive account of the pushes and pulls on the reader's attention. However, one might query why, beyond being quite interesting, it matters, as nothing of particular note appears to happen in this extract. This is because it is not until the young man finally meets his love, Norma, and offers her the flowers he is here about to buy, near the end of the tale, that the salience of this extract becomes apparent: not what is figured, but what is buried. It is often not possible to notice buried elements on a first reading of a text precisely because the reader is not supposed to notice them. As such, we would advocate being mindful of this when designing lessons (discussed further below).

When the young man goes to hand Norma the flowers, she does not recognise him. She tells him he must be mistaken. He reaches into his pocket, pulls out a hammer, and bludgeons her to death. We discover this is the fifth time this has happened. Typical reactions to this twist ending are shock and surprise (you can see these sentiments expressed, for example, in online reviews of the story). The reader experiences a 'rug pull' moment, realising that they haven't even been attributing the right genre to what seemed until the final reel to be a fairly sweet and gentle love story.

Upon rereading, the buried elements within the story begin to emerge. The text has utilised many of the strategies on Emmott and Alexander's (2014) list to discourage the reader from spotting them, but the reader can now discover the information was there all along.

For a start it was on the radio: the first item said, 'a hammer murderer was still on the loose'. This is the only time there is a specific mention of this however (Strategy 1: mention the item as little as possible). It is embedded within a very long sentence, essentially hiding it within the syntax (Strategy 2: use linguistic structures shown to reduce prominence). Here the sentence is so long and convoluted it would even be reasonable to suggest that for most people their working memory will be maxed out just trying to keep up with it.

Next, immediately following this 'news story' are another three, the next of which is 'JFK had declared that the situation in a little Asian country called Vietnam […] would bear watching' (Strategy 4: place the item next to one that is more prominent, so that the focus is on the latter). Here we have both a famous historical figure and a famous event to pull focus away from the hammer murderer, a story the reader is then even more likely to just dismiss as filler. Furthermore, King also plays a clever little trick by revealing more precisely the time at which the story is taking place through the item about Vietnam, encouraging the reader to focus on orienting the timeline – the war has not yet begun but is on the horizon – rather than worrying about anything in the story that came before (Strategy 7: place information in positions where the reader is distracted). This strategy is also utilised later, when the young man pauses and touches something in his pocket. Here the reader is being repeatedly encouraged to infer that the young man is the eponymous one 'who loved flowers', distracting their attention from wondering what the object in his pocket might be.

King also makes three innovative uses of negation to achieve Strategy 5 – 'make the item apparently unimportant in the narrative world' – as well as throwing a few others into the mix for good measure. First, the entire reel of news events is prefaced with the phrase 'the radio poured out bad news that no one listened to': the reader is told that whilst they are hearing this information, even the characters in the scene are not paying attention to it. Thus, in Stockwell's terms, the 'noisiness' of the radio as a potential attractor is dampened even before we hear it. This also arguably utilises Strategy 10: 'get the narrator […] to say that the item is uninteresting'. This is then reinforced at the close: 'none of it seemed real, none of it seemed to matter'. This final phrase is a particularly astute authorial tease in the use of the perception modal 'seemed' – a nudge to the rereader – as whilst it may 'seem' not to matter, it very much does. This use of negation is employed a final time later on where we are told 'the bad news *faded*', literally encouraging us to let the information we have just heard to decay from our memory: to 'fade'.

We hope that this analysis has first of all demonstrated the power of stylistic knowledge. Unlike approaches to studying fiction that are text specific – teaching students *about* a given text – stylistics equips us with tools that can then be applied to *any* text. This is not to suggest, of course, that knowledge about specific texts is not also at times incredibly valuable and important, but it is in most cases necessarily non-transferable. Accruing a 'stylistics toolkit' of knowledge, by contrast, enables an individual to analyse potentially any text. In this sense, we argue, stylistics is one of the most empowering means of analysis we can offer to students, as it quickly releases them from being dependent on an expert, their teacher, to be able to tackle texts independently.

Stylisticians see part of the skill of this kind of approach being situated in being able to select the most appropriate 'tool' for the job: not only being able to perform a figure-ground or a modality analysis, but to decide which approach is the best fit for the a given text or extract. This is not a book which simply aims to introduce stylistic frameworks, however, and we have decided that figure-ground configuration and burying are complementary frameworks ideally suited to reflect not just on the texts we study, but the context in which we study them: the English classroom.

Activities and Reflections

1. Figure-ground and burying can be a productive way of exploring genre expectations. Go back to the extract from 'The Man Who Loved Flowers' above. First, read it adopting the assumption it is a love story, then the assumption it is a horror story: how do these expectations influence what you figure and what you pass over?

2. Try this same process with a text you teach. Could you design an exercise like this to undertake with students for an extract, a poem, or even a whole novel?

3. Reflect with your students on the distinctions in what they notice and what they attribute salience to the first time they read a text compared to revisiting it as a rereader. You could even use this exercise as the basis of a discussion about first time and subsequent readings.

5.7 Attention in the classroom

We will now offer five examples of areas in which these frameworks – figure-ground and burying – can enable useful reflection on aspects of teaching and studying fiction.

5.7.1 Attention and text knowledge

In the previous section, we did spoil a plot event for you. Before we revealed this spoiler, however, we offered you the chance to avoid it by reading the story first. Some of you will have taken us up on this offer and others won't have, but every reader of this text was given the opportunity to make an informed choice. Such choices are not always offered, and are not always possible to offer, to students. However, we argue that close attention to the sequencing and framing of activities and the sharing of other information in lessons pertaining to the study of a fictional work, can preserve many features of authentic episodes of reading purely for enjoyment, without sacrificing academic rigour. In fact, we have tried to mimic and demonstrate that in our analysis above and encourage you to take a moment to reflect on it.

Assuming you were unfamiliar with 'The Man Who Loved Flowers', through the sequencing of passage and discussion, this book preserved the opportunity for you to read the extract for yourself before revealing the crucial piece of information that was necessary to explore how the concept of 'burying' was employed. Even after you read the passage, the analysis first walks through the patterns of attentional attraction before finally turning to discussing the knowledge from the end of the story that we had and, if you hadn't read it before, you did not. This, we argue, is a good example of how it is possible to structure the study of a work of fiction to allow for the most authentic reading experience that was possible in an education context (here, demonstrating a burying analysis). In other words, whilst acknowledging it is often impossible, even undesirable, to offer students an experience of a literary work that they are studying that fully mimics or recreates a 'reading for pleasure' experience, we posit that by paying attention to the structure and sequence of when things are introduced, it *is* achievable to align these two types of reading more closely.

There are myriad things studying fiction courses are asked to achieve, certainly more than is achievable in any one unit, and some things that can militate against one another. As such the space for authentic reading for enjoyment rapidly shrinks as students progress through school and for those older students in particular it would be reasonable to perceive units dedicated solely to engaging in reading for pleasure as a waste of extremely limited time. We do not dispute this. However, it is also important to remember that instilling a love of reading is one of the most powerful things that can be done to help ensure a young person's educational success. Even controlling for variables like household income, gender and level of parental education, reading for pleasure remains a better predictor of academic success than postcode (OECD 2010). As such, we posit that one of the best ways in which school English can foster this hugely powerful practice, whilst also serving the needs of national assessments, is to make studying fiction look and feel as much like reading for enjoyment as possible wherever it is reasonably practicable to do so. Often even a slight recalibration of the order of the tasks and some careful consideration of what happens when can dramatically alter the degree of synergy between the two.

5.7.2 Attention, immersion and transportation

Another complementary dimension of classroom practice that is important to think about through the lens of attention is immersion. Here are two reader reviews of another Stephen King novel, *The Outsiders*, taken from the website *Goodreads*:

1. King has done it again! The last time I was this enthralled with one of his books was *Finders Keepers*. While I do read a lot, it is not often I find a book that I don't want to put down at all. In fact, the biggest selling point is that I am in no way, shape or form a morning person. Dragging myself out of bed is the greatest challenge of my day. But, I woke up early, without an alarm, when I had about 100 pages to go because I was so into it I couldn't stop thinking about it and wanted to finish it! (Reader A)
2. Stephen King has done it again with a powerful story that pulls the reader into the middle and will not let them go. (Reader B)
   https://www.goodreads.com/book/show/36124936-the-outsider?from_choice=true

Both these readers describe the immersive power of reading King's novel. Reader A comments on being 'enthralled' by the book, not being able to 'put [it] down' and being 'unable to stop thinking about it. Reader B explicitly gives the book agency in that it 'pulls the reader' and 'will not let them go'. In cognitive psychology and linguistics, this sense of being lost in a book is known as transportation (Gerrig 1993), a metaphor used to conceptualise the reader as a traveller, and the text is the other world visited on their trip (reading). Gerrig explains that when a reader is transported into a story world, they become immersed in the fictional world and lose access to parts of the real world which may have two main consequences: first, a neglect of physical surroundings; and second, a lack of reference to other information held in memory.

Thus, in terms of figure-ground, immersion can be thought of as essentially an attentional zooming in: the text becomes such a strong figure that the rest of the world falls into the ground. This experience can of course vary in levels of intensity but it is not unusual for readers to lose track of everything from their physical space and environment to their sense of time. Readers might, for example, fail to notice someone entering or leaving the room, or that there has been a stark change in temperature or light. They might 'miss' minutes or even hours going by, thinking that a much shorter time has passed whilst they have been reading. Importantly, many readers report enjoying this sensation and even cite is as a central reason for their love of reading. Whilst there are studies that show this in concrete terms, enjoyment of immersion is evident in the everyday language used to describe reading for pleasure, like escapism, or 'getting lost in a good book'.

Gerrig also argues that when readers have highly immersive reading experiences, they are more likely to be in some way changed by that experience, as well as more likely to align their beliefs to those of the story world. This claim was later tested by Green and Brock (2000), who found that readers are more likely to accept, rather than critically consider, that conditions in story worlds hold true in the real world if they were highly transported when they were reading. They also found that

> greater transportation was systematically associated with a more positive evaluation of the main characters of a narrative [...] Transported individuals may have a greater affinity for story characters and thus may be more likely to be swayed by the feelings or belief expressed by those characters'
>
> (Green and Brock 2000: 719).

Effectively, then, greater transportation or 'transportability' involves readers displaying higher levels of emotional engagement, closer connections with the characters, and a greater potential for the story to have a powerful impact on the reader, who can be changed by their journey into the narrative world. This kind of experience can have positive implications. For example, Murphy et al. (2011) demonstrate that greater transportability can result in knowledge gain since readers invest significant amounts of their time in a text and may therefore be committed to change some aspect of their behaviour as a result of the knowledge they have acquired.

However, the research also problematises the benefits of being transported. In Green and Brock's study, for instance, participants were asked to read a story in which a young woman is murdered by a psychiatric patient. They found that readers who were highly transported by this story thought levels of violent crime were higher than those who were not transported and were more likely to say that psychiatric patients should not be allowed out unsupervised. In other words, the story made them think the world, and specifically those hospitalised as a result of mental illness, were more dangerous, and transportation reduced their ability to counter-argue or think more objectively about the central messages of the text. Marsh et al. (2012) also found that as fictional narratives are not always completely accurate (i.e. they may represent the world in ways that are incompatible with the real world), highly transported readers may acquire incorrect knowledge that can be difficult to shift and/or change their real-world knowledge to erroneously match the world of the story that they are reading. And Stockwell (2011) argues that greater investment may actually lead to greater feelings of vulnerability in a reader. We would suggest that this, in turn, may impact on an individual's ability to take a more objective, critical stance. With regards to studying fiction in the classroom, these studies raise important questions about how to get students to think critically about what they read.

Gerrig and Egidi (2010) explore this idea of criticality in detail by distinguishing between two types of processes that readers use when engaging with a text: intuitive processes and reflective processes. They argue that intuitive processes are automatic and occur without any real effort. They are natural, 'first impression' responses that we utilise for the majority of the time that we are reading. On the other hand, reflective processes are more considered and require careful thought and planning.

According to Gerrig and Egidi, a reflective reader will deliberately engage in critical processes that override the more natural intuitive responses to reading that may arise and will be able to move into a more critical mode of reading. Gerrig and Egidi stress that any reader may be both intuitive and reflective at different points of their reading, and that we all read in intuitive and reflective ways at different times and in different circumstances, with different texts and with different reasons for reading. They also point out that some texts encourage more or less reflective stances and that consequently, readers might shift from intuitive to reflective reading and vice versa as they move from book to book or even, for example, between different sections of the same novel. Gerrig and Egidi also suggest that through the language choices they make, authors themselves can influence when readers might choose to abandon more intuitive responses in favour of reflective ones, for example by drawing attention to moments of uncertainty and ambiguity, and deliberately foregrounding difficult questions. Some writers will naturally be more inclined to do this and consequently support readers to take more reflective stances.

Gerrig and Egidi also view literary analysis (in its broadest sense) as a controlled and reflective experience. They argue that 'most literary analysis arises from rereading rather than the initial reading of the text' (2010: 203). This also raises some interesting questions about how literary texts are introduced in the classroom. Since intuitive reading appears to be the default mode, a more reflective approach needs time (and good supporting activities) to develop: readers need time and space to be reflective since initial responses are always likely to be intuitive ones.

Activities and Reflections

1. How does reading take place in your classroom? Asking students to take turns reading the text out loud could divert their attention from the narrative and affect or break their sense of transportation, particularly at major plot points or emotionally engaging scenes, which research suggests may be best dealt with by facilitating transportation.

2. One possible consequence of transportation is that students may be less likely to think critically about a text. Following Gerrig and Egidi's research, consider how you could encourage a more critical stance through rereading and discussion. What else could you do to support this without disrupting the benefits that being transported does bring?

3. Engaging students in discussions about texts they find highly transporting is really important if reading might result in misguided beliefs. At the same time, immersive experiences are likely to be the ones students have found most powerful and enjoyable. How can we encourage young people to think critically about and question popular texts, including those that they might read outside of school?

Research suggests there are other benefits to immersion beyond simple enjoyment. In essence, this kind of transportation involves higher levels of emotional engagement in texts, closer connections with the characters, and a greater potential for the story to have a powerful impact on the reader, who can be changed by their journey into the narrative world (Green and Brock 2000). These, it is uncontroversial to suggest, are all positive features of reading it would be good for young people to experience. For those who don't typically read for pleasure in their leisure time this is especially important, as they are unlikely to have experienced this sensation in relation to books, though they may well have felt it whilst gaming or watching television or films (Csikszentmihalyi 1996, 2014).

In the classroom, therefore, it is useful to think about and reflect on what capacity lesson designs offer students to become immersed in the story, as and when this is something we would like to achieve. Such strong figuring of the world of the text that it prompts students to be transported can be a powerful tool in turning young people on to the joys of reading. We would suggest a number of things which teachers might find useful to consider, both when teaching class readers, but also when thinking about whether or not, and how, to instigate discussions with students about books they read for pleasure:

- Anything within the classroom which competes with the text for the student's attention leaves them less equipped to become immersed in the story because it carries an attentional cost. For example, asking students to take turns reading the text out loud. Here, they are being asked to toggle their attention between the 'real world' and the 'narrative world' level as they monitor when it will be their turn. This is particularly salient when considering major plot points or emotionally engaging scenes, which we argue may be best dealt with by facilitating transportation to maximise students' investment in and enjoyment of the story. Ways to achieve this could include dealing with these portions of a narrative in one go without fragmentation, saving questions or tasks until after reading is complete and, or, by the teacher reading these parts of the text to the class.
- If students have been highly immersed in the story, they are likely to be actively disoriented at the point reading concludes and they re-access the world of the classroom. This means that time to process and acknowledge this involvement with the story world may well be gratefully received. In everyday reading some people refer to this as a 'book hangover' – the feeling that a bit of time is needed to 'get over' what has just been read before being ready to critically reflect on it or do something else. A moment of quiet reflection or shared reorienting through open discussion could be fruitful ways in which to honour this experience with students. Equally, trying to immediately follow this kind of immersed reading with a highly structured task may well breed resentment towards the task type itself. For example, asking students to write a PEE paragraph[2] about Gatsby's swim, Piggy's fall, or Boxer's trip to the vets when they have just read this for the first time probably won't do PEE paragraphs any favours.
- If students are successfully transported by a story, they are likely not to have thought critically about it because their attention was fully focused on experiencing the narrative. They are therefore likely to need time after reading to reflect on what they've read in order to think critically about it. This suggests that open discussion after reading might better prepare students to analyse the text rather than asking for critical interpretations immediately.
- People who are highly transported by a text often describe an inability to put the book down and a compulsion to keep reading – this is worth considering if it is ever practically possible to allow students to take copies of their class readers away from the classroom with them. Alternatively, this is a good thing to take into account when deciding how to section

up the reading of the text across lessons: points at which you would be willing to put your bookmark back in are typically good stopping points; places where you would leave your light on and carry on reading even when you knew it would make you tired in the morning are probably best avoided!

Closely related to this is the consideration of how best to deal with those elements of the plot that teachers know are coming, but which students may be oblivious to or blindsided by as first-time readers.

5.7.3 Foreshadowing, twists and reveals

A third area where reflecting on attention is valuable is in relation to the plots of studied texts. For teachers who have taught a text several times and studied it in detail, instances of foreshadowing can seem overwhelmingly obvious. Lenny accidentally killing his pet mouse by stroking it too hard in *Of Mice and Men* for many teachers may as well have a big flashing sign over it screaming 'This is not going to end well!' So too it now feels so obvious to us, as rereaders of 'The Man Who Loved Flowers', that the young man is the hammer murderer. This is a phenomenon that will have happened to most people at some point when rereading or rewatching a story with a twist: suddenly it seems genuinely hard to fathom how you could not work it out the first time, and all the hints and clues now seem to be obvious. This feeling can be explained as the difference in the narrative schema of a rereader compared to that of a first-time reader.

5.7.4 Attention and narrative schemas

As discussed extensively in Chapter 4, a narrative schema is a reader's mental version of the text. Thus, the narrative schemas of first-time readers will contain only the story as they have read it so far, with things that have been figured for them likely to inform its contents and things that have remained in the ground potentially entirely absent. For rereaders, their narrative schema is likely to offer a much richer source of knowledge, information, responses and emotions. To continue Emmott and Alexander's burying metaphor, rereaders have the opportunity to comb through their narrative schema, isolating parts and examining them. For first-time readers – unless their narrative schema has been prematurely populated by discourse about the sections of text they are yet to read – these elements remain hidden. This fundamental disjunct in text knowledge between teacher and students of course presents many opportunities, but it also carries risks.

One example is the temptation to highlight the concept of foreshadowing when reading a story with students for the first time. By its very nature foreshadowing can only truly be recognised after at least one complete reading has taken place; foreshadowed elements are effectively buried elements. We may *suspect* that something in an earlier chapter has been positioned there as foreshadowing of later events but we cannot *confirm* this until we reach that later event. Thus, to designate something as foreshadowing to a class who, we presume, have never come across it before, is to unjustly exert the teacher's power of knowledge over them. Unjustly, because this power comes as a result of being the reader in the room who is further ahead. This is ultimately no different to the friend in the playground making the other children bring them things under threat of spoiling which character dies in the next episode of *Game of Thrones*.

In one sense we are of course being hyperbolic here, but this is to highlight how intolerant we typically are of this sort of behaviour in any context other than the classroom; it is worth, therefore, considering this scenario first as a reader, rather than a teacher. There are, of course, no easy solutions to this, but we would suggest that being aware and mindful of this difficult balancing act is important.

> **Activities and Reflections**
>
> 1. Think about the last twist or reveal you encountered that shocked, surprised or delighted you. Now imagine before you got there, someone who had read the book or seen the film already just came and told it to you. How would you feel?
> 2. Choose a text you like to teach. How do you deal with foreshadowing, buried elements, twists and reveals? In light of this chapter is there anything you want to change moving forwards. Why? Why not?

5.7.5 Pre-figuring

Another way in which figure-ground relationships and burying can be helpfully extended to a discourse level, is deploying them to investigate how the organisation of the classroom and the interactions that occur within it might be understood. In short, it's very easy for teachers (as with writers) to manipulate what becomes the figure and what is relegated to the ground. This can happen when teachers set up tasks that ask students to view a text or an idea from a particular point of view. Similar to noticing foreshadowing, pre-figuring necessarily stems from the teacher's status as a rereader of the text.

Classrooms are also dynamic spaces where many other factors can influence what gets given prominence. Wall displays, posters and handouts of examination board assessment criteria and key words, and writing frames (e.g. PEE/PEA paragraphs) might also pre-figure certain ways of thinking and legitimising interpretations.

> **Activities and Reflections**
>
> 1. Choose one of your lessons. Looking through any plans and resources, can you see any instances of pre-figuring. Why are they there? Do they need to be? Can you think of a way to rejig the lesson to avoid unnecessary pre-figuring?
> 2. Are there are certain contexts in which pre-figuring is pedagogically appropriate?
> 3. Think about displays you have seen in classrooms (yours or others'). Are displays put up because they're attractive and eye-catching, or because they contain the latest 'buzz words'? What do they say about what a teacher's values, the books they read and the kinds of official and unofficial documentation that is foregrounded? How might they be responsible for pointing students towards what's considered to be important in the classroom? Do the classroom walls reinforce particular pedagogical messages?

Further reading

Comprehensive and accessible accounts of figure-ground can be found in Gibbons and Whiteley (2018) and Stockwell (2020). An account of this cognitive poetic framework that is suitable for students is available in Giovanelli and Mason (2018a). The concept of burying is introduced in Sanford and Emmott (2012) and extended and further applied in Emmott and Alexander (2014). Pre-figuring is introduced in Giovanelli and Mason (2015) and elaborated in Mason and Giovanelli (2017). The idea of transportation is fully covered in Gerrig (1993). Aside from the research mentioned in this chapter, a good recent overview of work with plenty of summaries of empirical studies on immersion can be found in Hakemulder et al. (2017).

Notes

1 This is not related to the notion of preferred learning styles, sometimes called 'VAK', an idea which has now been debunked as not scientifically sound.
2 Point Evidence Explanation paragraph.

6
READERS

This chapter will:

- provide an overview of reader-response theories with a focus on Louise Rosenblatt's transactional theory;
- introduce and discuss the cognitive linguistic reader-response framework Text World Theory;
- examine *relevance* in relation to text choices and developing students' critical responses.

6.1 Reading as response

Here are four reviews, taken from www.Amazon.co.uk of Paula Hawkins' (2015) best-selling novel *The Girl on the Train*.

READER A: I found myself totally engrossed in the mystery of it. I was able to get to the bottom of it in the latter stages but this didn't take away from my enjoyment of the story or the mechanics of the writing.

READER B: great thriller that keeps you guessing as to whose [sic] done it, while keeping you on the edge of your seat with many twists & turns.

READER C: One of the poorest and most predictable plots that I have ever read. Besides the poor development of the characters and the irritating tone of the book, it was obvious fairly early on in the book what the ending would be.

READER D: Badly written, boring, predictable.

These comments demonstrate how readers may respond to a text in very different – and here extreme – ways. Although they largely focus on similar aspects of the novel, such as its structure, Hawkins' style and characterisation, and the emotional effects on them as readers, these readers report a set of differing experiences of the book; it is also clear that interpretations are not simply transmitted along a chain from author to reader. In this chapter we draw on this important concept to examine the role of the reader in making meaning. We focus on the centrality of the reader in the interpretative process and highlight the importance of teachers thinking about the kinds of knowledge and other resources that readers both bring to and need to access in the literature classroom.

Here is another example of how readers make meaning, this time from Stanley Fish's (1980) book *Is There a Text in this Class?* Fish tells the story of an undergraduate seminar where he had left the following list of authors, used as reading list for a previous class, on the board.

> Jacobs-Rosenbaum
> Levin
> Thorne
> Hayes
> Ohman (?)

(Fish 1980: 323)

Fish had drawn a box around the names, written 'p. 43' next to the box and informed his students, who had been studying seventeenth-century religious poetry, that the 'text' was a religious poem with the instruction that they should analyse it. Unsurprisingly, the students' interpretations were grounded in what they had been studying, including comments on the religious significance of the names (Jacob's Ladder, the crown of thorns, the tribe of Levi, 'Ohman' read as 'amen') and the structure of the 'poem' with its three Hebrew names, two Christian and the ambiguous 'Ohman' (the question mark was in fact because Fish had forgotten how to spell the name 'Ohmann'). One student even counted the total number of letters in the names and realised than the three most common ones were 'S', 'O', and 'N'; needless to say, the students had taken it upon themselves to the poem as a religious allegory. Fish highlights how the students' responses to the 'poem' must have been influenced not by the text itself but rather by being told that the text was a poem. In other words, the names and the context of the classroom evoked various types of a RELIGIOUS POETRY schema that the students then used to help them interpret the poem. As Fish (1980: 326) argues:

> In other words, acts of recognition, rather than being triggered by formal characteristics, are their source. It is not that the presence of poetic qualities compels a certain kind of attention but that the paying of a certain kind of attention results in the emergence of poetic qualities. As soon as my students were aware that it was poetry they were seeing, they began to look with poetry-seeing eyes, that is, with eyes that saw everything in relation to the properties they knew poems to possess.

As both examples demonstrate, what a text means is largely how readers *respond* to that text. As in Example 1, readers may interpret the same words in very different ways justifying their reading in terms of preference and emotional response. And, as in Example 2, readers may impose specific ways of reading onto a text, in this instance framed within certain institutional parameters and expectations. Fish uses the term 'interpretive communities' (1980: 14) to show how readers' own responses arise through membership of larger social groups with conventional ways of looking at texts and with categories (e.g. 'literature', 'poetry') through which readings are then framed. In both cases, readers are responsible for generating meaning; meaning is not simply there to be found.

6.2 Reader-response theories and education

There are various theories of reading that highlight the importance of the reader. These theories are fairly recent and stand in contrast to two other ways of thinking about meaning in a text.

In the first, literary critics in the nineteenth and early twentieth century focused on the author as the source of a text's meaning and attached importance to extra-textual (biography, history) detail. In the second, critics working around the mid twentieth century shifted the focus on to the text as a self-contained entity, most notably in a practice that came to be known as *New Criticism* (e.g. Brooks 1947; Welleck and Warren 1949). New Critics generally viewed both knowledge about the author and the reader's emotional response as irrelevant to the study of literature (although New Critics tended to focus largely on poetry). Reading – or deciphering – a poem was largely about working out a meaning that resided in its internal structure and could be deduced from a close and careful analysis of its oppositions and tensions; the poem in effect was an autonomous entity.

Over the last 50 years or so, advances in literary and cultural theory, in linguistics, and in psychology and cognitive science have led to ideas that aim to account more explicitly for the role of the reader without necessarily dismissing the author and the text. Beach (1993) draws attention to five separate theorisations of reader-response that have been particularly influential in educational contexts. Although written some time ago, Beach's list still provides a useful overview of the range of reader-response theories that exist. We list these below with some added discussion of each.

1. **Textual theories**: these examine how readers draw on explicit knowledge about language, structure and genre to make meaning. For example, a reader might use their understanding of the conventions of the thriller genre to guide their way through the latest Gillian Flynn novel, expecting certain types of character and plot features and being responsive to particular aspects of style. In this instance, exposure to Flynn's work and a wider range of thriller novels is likely to lead to a different kind of response than a reader who has hardly encountered the genre. Textual theories also suggest that an understanding of the conventions of different semiotic systems and/or understanding of textual allusions shape and influence responses. These theories emphasise that language of the text presents a system of gaps (Iser 1974), which are fleshed out by the reader's background knowledge and active meaning-making to provide a coherent reading. They can also, however, often assume a target or 'implied' (Booth 1983) reader or a 'model' (Eco 1979) or 'super' (Riffaterre 1959) reader equipped with the knowledge required to understand a text. As such these can ignore the reality of a 'real' reader and the influence of emotion, culture and society on the ways that texts are interpreted.
2. **Experiential theories**: these examine how readers interact on a personal level with a text. For example, readers bring a whole series of emotional 'baggage' (feelings, past experiences, emotions) to reading and this baggage plays an important role in influencing interpretations as they make connections between the text and their own lives. Readers also invest their energies into constructing imaginative worlds, immersing themselves into plots, siding with characters and developing empathetic and ethical responses. Reading therefore becomes a platform for personal growth (see DESWO 1989) through emotional interaction and the experience of literature (Rosenblatt 1978). One criticism of extreme versions of these theories is that they may promote responses that are typically naïve and at a distance from the text itself: for example, a student may choose to foreground a simple personal response to a poem, for example arguing that Wordsworth's 'Daffodils' is a poem simply about feeling joy at seeing some beautiful flowers.
3. **Psychological theories**: these examine how cognitive and psychological processes (including personality) influence meaning. For example, young readers differ from adults in terms

of their life experiences, how they think and the ways in which they can manage their emotions (Goswami 2007) and so, typically, are different kinds of readers (Nikolajeva 2014). In turn, these attributes increase as a young reader ages so that reading may be viewed as part of a developmental process or series of stages (e.g. Appleyard 1990). These theories may also draw on models of psychoanalysis (Holland 1973) and personality to account for the ways in which the minds of readers interact with texts. Although these theories draw on work in cognitive science, some earlier ideas may not be as sensitive to social contexts as more recent advances in the field. Equally, some psychoanalytical models have shifted the basis of meaning entirely onto the reader so that the text itself becomes an irrelevance. We shall return specifically to this point in our discussion of Text World Theory in Section 6.4.

4. **Social theories**: these examine how the social contexts in which reading takes place influence interpretation. For example, interactions in the classroom are a very specific type of institutional discourse with clearly defined socially-orientated roles (teacher, student) and differences in power and expected behaviours (e.g. a teacher asks a question, a student responds). Viewing the reading experience simply through a 'social' lens can, however, lose sight of the influence of personal as well as wider cultural factors that influence reading.
5. **Cultural theories**: these examine how readers' larger cultural values and membership of particular groups influence reading. For example, readers may respond to texts based on their belief systems, ideologies and wider language practices, as well as specific values and experiences from their own cultures. Fish's notion of an 'interpretive community' discussed earlier in this chapter is essentially a combination of social and cultural theories of reading; here, Fish draws attention to how stances towards reading and interpretation are conditioned and framed by larger societal and cultural values and group membership.

Activities and Reflections

1. As a starting point, think about which of the theories outlined above you most agree with or find attractive. Are there any that you don't like, or feel are useful?
2. Consider the extent to which your ideas about reading shape your current practice. For example, would you naturally give more prominence to a textual theory of reading? To what extent are others marginalised or downplayed?
3. To what extent do Fish's comments on the ways that literature is framed influence the kinds of responses that students provide to texts? Does reading fiction in the classroom always have to result in a 'literary reading' or should more 'recreational' forms of reading also be encouraged? (See Mackey (2019) for discussion of these terms and our discussion of emotions in Chapter 8).

6.3 Louise Rosenblatt's transactional theory

One key experiential theory that has become very influential (particularly in the United States) is Rosenblatt's transactional theory (Rosenblatt 1938, 1978). Rosenblatt's theory, in many ways a proto-cognitive one that was developed over a number of years, was a reaction against both predominantly author-centred and text-centred approaches that marginalised the role of the reader in making meaning. Transactional theory aims to 'admit into the limelight the whole scene

– author, text and reader' (Rosenblatt 1978: 5). Indeed, unlike many reader-response theories, Rosenblatt emphasises how meaning is co-constructed between author and reader through the text. As she argues, 'the author has selected these words and no others as the cues that will guide the reader's performance' (1978: 15); and '[the reader] will have a sense of achieved communication, sometimes, indeed, of communion with the author' (1978: 50).

Rosenblatt draws on the work of the social scientists John Dewey and Arthur F. Bentley to propose that reading 'comes into being in the live circuit set up between the reader and the "text"' (1978: 14) as part of a 'structured experience' (1978: 66) that fleshes out the literary work. She uses the term 'transaction' (as opposed to 'interaction') to show that the reader and text are integrated parts of a unified phenomenon: the very essence of text *must* assume a reader. Reading is thus 'an event in time' (1978: 12) in which the language of the text cues up aspects of a reader's knowledge that are used to start to develop meaning. Equally, Rosenblatt is keen to stress that the act of reading is an on-going and dynamic process and that interpretations and meanings can never be fixed. Rereadings and discussions with others are therefore an important part of how we build up our experiences with texts: across the various readings, readers may embellish or reject certain interpretations, backtrack and revise their thoughts and draw on both previous knowledge and new sources of information as they read, reread and reflect on their responses.

The language of the text itself acts to 'regulate' (1978: 11) the type of knowledge that is useful in the emerging interpretation so that as reading progresses, less salient information and ideas can be revised and/or rejected. Since literary transactions are influenced by various kinds of background knowledge that readers bring with them (e.g. memories, past experiences, age, and so on), even readers from a similar background may interpret texts in slightly nuanced ways. Equally, returning to a particular text later in life may result in a very different type of reading. For example, an adult reader is likely to interpret *Hamlet* in ways that are different to when they read it at school as a teenager.

Rosenblatt distinguishes between different kinds of reading that arise as a result of the reader's 'focus of attention' (1978: 23). She labels those readings that are largely concerned with acquiring information as 'efferent' (1978: 24) (from the Latin *efferre*: to carry away). In contrast, 'aesthetic' (1978: 24) readings are geared towards a more felt experience, an awareness of the text as a work of art (Fish's 'religious poem' is a good example of this) and often reflect the reader emotional engagement during the reading event itself. In fact, although Rosenblatt initially conceives of the two stances as separate types of experience, she later positions them as extremes on a continuum and argues that most reading is likely to occur towards the middle of the continuum and that readers will naturally divert their attention and take particular stances towards one of the two ends depending on the nature of the reading task ahead of them. These stances are also influenced by the situation and circumstances of reading and, in a classroom, potentially by the approach taken by the teacher. In other words, teaching activities can promote *more* or *less* aesthetic or efferent stances.

We return to these issues in our discussion of Text World Theory in Section 6.4. For now, it is worth considering the fact that activities which lead to a reader, on the one hand, to adopt a more efferent reading stance may well lead to students retrieving learnt interpretations (from teachers or elsewhere) and knowing *about* the text rather than the text itself (see our discussion of this in Chapter 2). On the other hand, clearly, it is desirable for information (in whatever shape or form) to be retained to support interpretation itself and to inform tasks (presentations, summaries, essays and so on) at the end of a reading event. The key seems to be in a sense of balance, which might in itself arise as a result of students' own awareness of how literary interpretation comes about: knowing *about* texts should never be a substitute for students being taught *how* to do literary analysis.

Activities and Reflections

1. Think about the different kinds of texts that you teach. Do some of them lend themselves to more or less aesthetic and/or efferent stances? To what extent might a more efferent stance be useful when discussing literature?
2. How do Rosenblatt's ideas on stance relate to our discussion of authentic and manufactured reading in Chapter 2? For example, could 'aesthetic' equate to 'authentic' or is this too simplistic a way of explaining these positions?
3. How important is prior knowledge when it comes to reading and studying fiction?

6.4 Text World Theory

6.4.1 The basics of Text World Theory

We have outlined Rosenblatt's transactional theory above firstly because of its influence on English education and, by consequence, the thinking of English teachers and secondly because we see very clear connections between Rosenblatt's ideas and the framework we now turn to. That framework is Text World Theory (Werth 1999; Gavins 2007), which is grounded in empirical findings from cognitive psychology and cognitive linguistics, and has evolved into a flexible and insightful way of thinking about human communication.

Text World Theory is a cognitive discourse grammar: *cognitive* in that it is concerned with describing the ways that we process information; *discourse* in that it is sensitive to context. The theory provides a unified and consistent way of examining how rich fictional worlds are co-constructed between author and reader, the role of the language of the text itself in those representations, and the ways in which readers may respond to texts, positioning themselves emotionally and ethically and so on.

Text World Theory proposes a number of conceptual layers to the reading experience (we have simplified these layers and some of the terminology associated with the model for practical purposes).

1. **The discourse-world**: the context in which reading takes place, which includes the situation of reading, and background information and knowledge brought to the event by the reader.
2. **Text-worlds**: these build up the fictional world in terms of time, location, characters and are developed through instances of actions and events. Text-worlds are constructed on the basis of textual cues and fleshed out by a reader's relevant background knowledge. Shifts in time and space trigger world-switches where readers' attention is diverted to a new set of actions and events.
3. **Additional-worlds**: these also divert attention but, crucially, this time to remote, as yet unrealised text-worlds (e.g. due to modality), or those which present a particular point of view. We shall return to these structures in Section 6.4.3.

As an example of Text World Theory in action, read the extract below taken from Susan Hill's *The Small Hand*. In this extract, the narrator has just come across a deserted house in the country and stops to investigate.

> I touched the cold iron latch. It lifted. I pushed. The gate was stuck fast. I put my shoulder to it and it gave a little and rust flaked away at the hinges. I pushed harder and slowly the gate moved, scraping on the ground, opening, opening. I stepped through it and I was inside. Inside a large, overgrown, empty, abandoned garden. To one side, steps led to a terrace and the house.
>
> Hill (2010: 13)

The starting point for Text World Theory is always the discourse-world, the immediate context in which reading takes place. A reader coming to the novel in 2020 is removed in time and place from the author (the novel was written in 2010). Unlike face-to-face communication, the vast majority of interaction with a written literary text will be similar. Text World Theory uses the term 'split discourse-world' (Gavins 2007: 26) to take account of the fact that the contexts of production and reception are different. In the context of reading, the reader constructs a mental version of their co-participant, here Susan Hill, that they use to guide their reading (see Chapter 7 for more on this). This may include various kinds of knowledge about her, her writing (knowledge that she writes ghost stories and detective thrillers for example) as well as knowledge gained from buying the book, reading the blurb on the back, reviews of the book, others talking about the book, and so on. Of course, this knowledge will differ from reader to reader but it is clear that readers bring a significant amount of information to the reading event with them and that all of this feeds into their engagement with the text.

As reading progresses, mental representations of the events described are built up. Like Rosenblatt's transactional theory, Text World Theory asserts that all of these mental representations (called text-worlds) are negotiated between the author, and reader. In other words, the reader acts on language cues in the text (placed there by the author) to activate various knowledge frames in order to build up meaning. In this sense, Text World Theory takes a broadly encyclopaedic approach to knowledge in that words act as reference points to stores of knowledge. In this instance, a word like 'house', although holding a conventional and shared meaning will also have more idiosyncratic meanings based on embodied encyclopaedic knowledge that has been experienced over time. For example, part of the meaning of 'house' will reside in the houses we have lived in, visited, seen on television and so on. Given that we have a tremendous amount of knowledge stored in long-term memory, crucially it is the language of the text itself that acts as a kind of safety valve to ensure that only required knowledge is called on. In Text World Theory this is known as 'the principle of text-drivenness' (Werth 1999: 140).

6.4.2 Building and developing text-worlds

In reading this extract, a reader acts on a set of instructions. It's as though a mental construct of the author, Susan Hill is effectively saying to her reader 'Imagine this context: there is a narrator who has arrived at a house and this is what he describes to us – go!'. This is the process of building text-worlds.

Encountering this extract, a reader first has to assume the position of the narrating 'I', since the events in the extract are experienced from his perspective and he is our only source of information on the events in the narrative. This means that we align our attention to the narrator's, understanding that the representation that we build up of the text-world is one informed by this perspective. This is so common with literary texts that we barely notice that we are doing it. As we build up this representation, we can identify two important kinds of information that we use. The first are known as world-building elements. These are the parts of the narrative that point out aspects of time, place, characters and objects. In the extract from *The Small Hand*, we can identify these as follows:

Time = some point in the past
Place = White House
Character = narrator
Objects = gate/latch

As we read, our representation of the scene develops as a result of secondary information. This information may be in the form of nouns that act as further world-builders such as 'shoulder', 'rust' and 'hinges', and verbs that add description or else propel the narrative forward through denoting actions: in Text World Theory, verbs form function-advancing propositions.

Here, we can see that the majority of function-advancing propositions in the first part of the extract relate to actions: 'touched', 'lifted', 'pushed', 'put', 'gave', 'flaked away', pushed', 'moved', 'scraping', 'opening', 'stepped through'. In other words, the mental representation of the scene is dynamic rather than static; one possible interpretation of this taxonomy of verbs is that it evokes a quick-paced atmosphere. Even in the final two sentences, which appear to be more descriptive, the clause 'steps led to a terrace and a house' impose a sense of movement through the verb 'led' on a scene that is stationary (in cognitive linguistics this is known as 'fictive motion' – see Talmy (2000)).

6.4.3 Text-world diagrams

Text World Theory often makes use of diagrams to demonstrate how a narrative develops. Diagrams are useful because they can outline some complex structures in more accessible ways. Pedagogically, they also provide an excellent way of allowing students to engage with and analyse the structure of texts in ways that conventional descriptions do not always do. We return to this second point in Section 6.4.4 but here we present an initial text-world diagram of the extract

Initial text-world ─── Point of view world

WB
time: the past
place: White House
characters: the narrator
objects: gate/latch

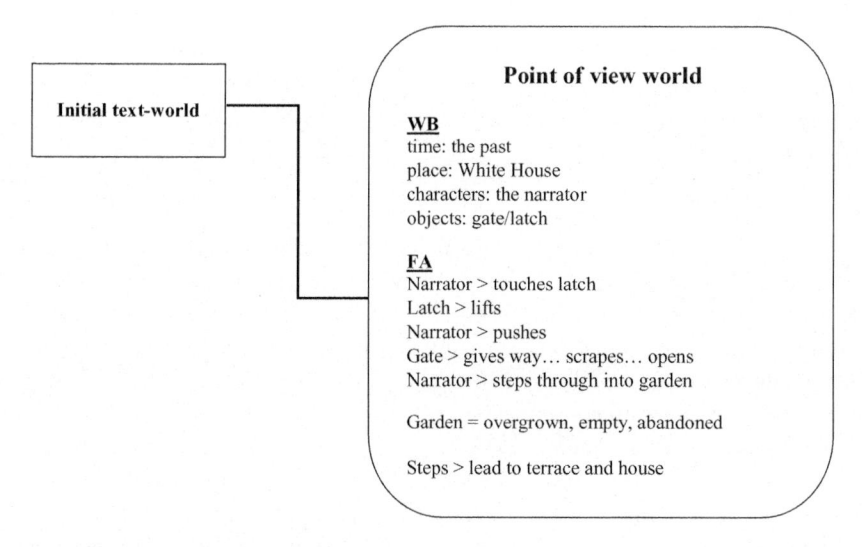

FA
Narrator > touches latch
Latch > lifts
Narrator > pushes
Gate > gives way… scrapes… opens
Narrator > steps through into garden

Garden = overgrown, empty, abandoned

Steps > lead to terrace and house

FIGURE 6.1 Text-world of *The Small Hand*

from *The Small Hand*. In this diagram, we have adapted some of terminology from the original theory by referring to the text-world created by the narrator's perspective as a 'Point of view' world, and by marking action verbs with '>' and descriptive verbs with '=' (Figure 6.1).

6.4.4 Shifts in world-structure

In the extract we have just been looking at, the structure is largely straightforward. The 'point of view' that we highlighted is a very common kind of shift in which some aspect of the original text-world (in this case the narrative perspective) is altered. In these cases, our attention is diverted away from the original text-world into a new mental representation that will differ to some degree in terms of its world-building elements. This shift is effectively a figure-ground reversal (see Chapter 5). A new figure (the new text-world) moves to become the focus of attention and original text-world is now the ground. This configuration has the potential to be permanent, as the new text-world becomes the new default one, or temporary, if there is a further shift either back to original world or to a new one.

There are different kinds of shifts and again we have simplified the original theory for practical reasons here. In addition to shifts in point of view, shifts may occur as a result of:

- direct/indirect speech or thought which introduces words or thoughts from a new perspective
- modality, hypotheticality, metaphor and negation, all of which ask a reader to conceptualise an alternative state of affairs

As an example of this in action, here is another extract from *The Small Hand*, which is taken from just after the section we previously looked at. At this moment in the novel, the narrator is reflecting on the strange sense he has about the house and his unexplained desire to find out more; he thinks of returning to the house in the daylight to 'uncover what was concealed, reveal what had been hidden. Find out why' (2010: 14) and wonders if he should do so.

> I might not have returned. Most probably, by the time I had made my way back to the main road, as of course I would, and reached London and my comfortable flat, the White House and what I had found there in the dusk of that late evening would have receded to the back of my mind and before long been quite forgotten. Even if I had come this way I might well never have found it again.
>
> (Hill 2010: 14)

In this extract, the narrator initially uses a modal verb 'might' and a negator 'not': 'I might not have returned'. Modality generally triggers text-worlds that contain as yet unrealised content (beliefs, wishes, desires, obligations and so on). Here the narrator contemplates a situation that is different to the one that happened. The modality here is supported by negation, a strong attractor, which places the negative counterpart of an utterance as the figure against the ground of its positive version. In other words, to conceptualise a negative, we first have to think of the positive version and then background it: a famous example is the phrase 'Don't think of an elephant' where it's impossible to conceptualise not thinking of an elephant without first thinking of an elephant! (Lakoff 2004) Since negation draws attention to absence, any one of its possible linguistic realisations will cue a shift across text-worlds. In this instance, we conceptualise a world in which the narrator does return and then negate this world.

More modality occurs through the modal adverb 'probably'. Here the text-world triggered is built up through a series of world-builders framed within the narrator's belief: he returns to the main road, goes back to London and his flat there and forgets about the White House. This replaces the original text-world until a final shift, this time framed around a hypothetical 'if' clause, removed in time and space from the original text-world and containing both modality and negation 'I might well have never found it again'. This text-world thus contains details of the narrator's thoughts on the possibility of being unable to relocate White House if he did choose to return.

All in all, this extract demands a great deal of a reader in terms of focusing attention on different entities at different times, and conceptualising various – and largely unrealised – scenes. In the context of the novel, this part of the chapter is an important one since the narrator's wandering mind is brought back to reality and his current location when he feels a ghostly presence outside the house with him. The increasing remoteness from the original text-world followed by movement back results in a series of shifts in attention for the reader before a sustained focus on the house and the climax of the chapter. In diagrammatic form, shown in Figure 6.2, the complexity

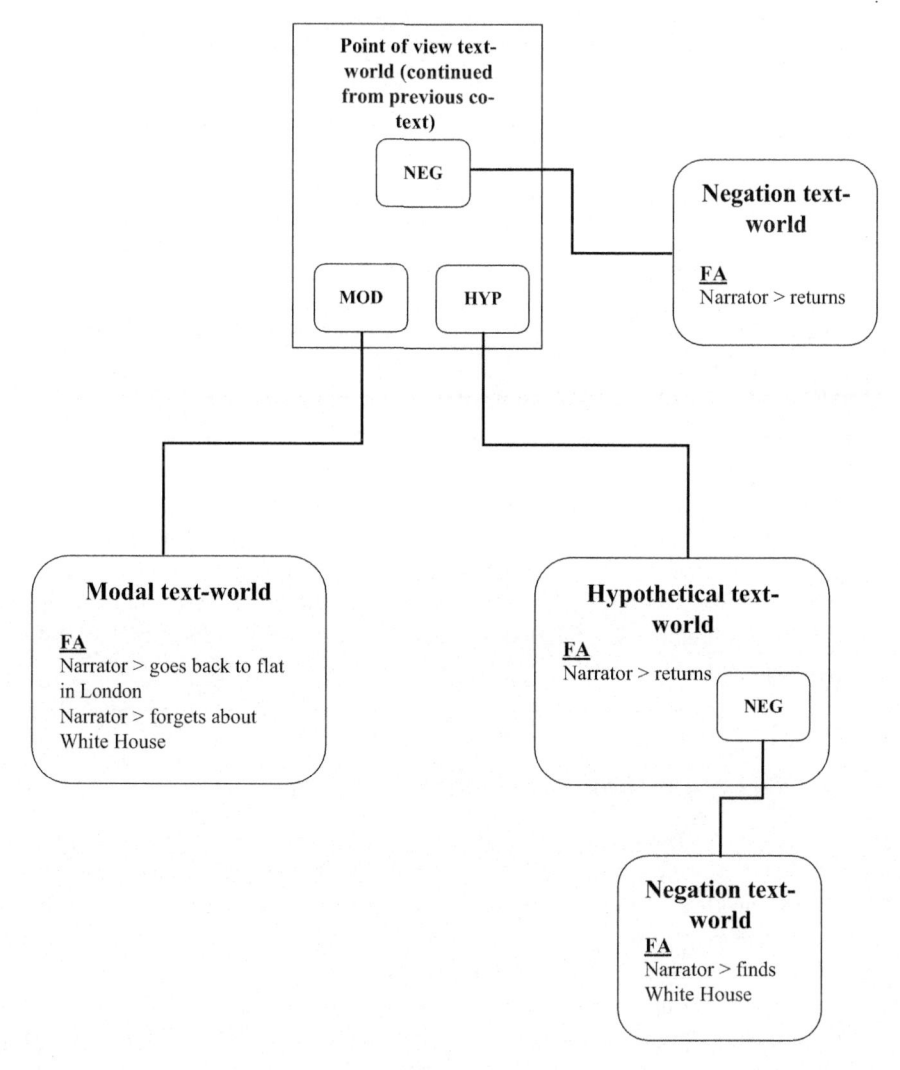

FIGURE 6.2 Remote text-worlds in *The Small Hand*

74 Readers

of this scene is spread out and made more explicit. Arguably, this provides a clearer way of demonstrating the nuances of the text's structure than would be possible through an analysis using words alone.

Activities and Reflections

1. Text World Theory can be used a descriptive grammar for the analysis of different genres (e.g. horror, science-fiction, romance). Use the framework to explore the ways in which texts use different kinds of function-advancing propositions (e.g. actions or states) at different points and for different effects. For example, here's another description of a spooky house, this time from a book written for children

   > I always paused at the gate to look at the house, which stood on its own little hillock as many churches do, and indeed there was something for the graveyard in its walled garden and something of the church in its arched Gothic windows and its spikes and ornaments. The garden gate was as much need of oil as the kissing gate and the latch so heavy that it took all my boyish strength to lift it; the metal so cold and damp it chilled my fingers to the bone.
   >
   > (Priestley 2007: 5)

2. Text World Theory can be used to explore writing for different audiences: ask students to undertake a re-write of *The Small Hand* for (teenagers/young/very young) children. What changes to the text would they make? What schematic knowledge might they aim to draw on? Would they make the text more or less complex? How and why? What happens if it becomes a picture book for pre-readers?

3. Rob Pope's (1995: 17–8) notions of included participants (explicitly stated characters, e.g. the narrator of *The Small Hand*) and excluded participants (characters not mentioned but assumed to have been present at some point in the fictional world but aren't 'captured' in Hill's text, e.g. the maker of the gate, the builder of the house, the ex-gardener, previous visitors) can be used for more radical re-writings of the base text. These ideas encourage students to shift point of view and deictic parameters. What do they now include in their writing – and what do they leave out?

6.4.5 Using Text World Theory: implications for practice

There are several ways in which Text World Theory can be used in the classroom. First, teachers could explicitly teach some key aspects of Text World Theory as a way of developing linguistic and literary awareness and supporting the analysis of texts. Short extracts which have interesting stylistic features such as the prominence of description and various layers of remote conceptualisations like those in *The Small Hand* lend themselves very well to a text-worlds analysis.

The use of diagrams can support students to examine the structure of texts and also has the potential to be used in different ways such as teacher summaries of poems and revision materials. This diagrammatic nature of Text World Theory thus has the potential for exploiting dual coding

(Paivio 1971, 1986; and see Caviglioni 2019 for recent applications in the classroom). Research that focuses on the explicit teaching of Text World Theory to aid student analysis can be found in Giovanelli (2010) (First World War poetry) and Giovanelli (2014) (advertising). Cushing (2018) examines how teachers used Text World Theory to teach grammatical concepts, highlighting the fact that a more conceptual approach (for example using the idea of 'world-builders' to explore noun phrases) offers a way of avoiding a terminology-led approach to literary reading that can result in superficial or minimal learning.

Since Text World Theory is a cognitive reader-response theory, a third way in which it may be useful for the teacher is in supporting the design of teaching activities themselves. Indeed, we would suggest that one of the key affordances of Text World Theory is that it is a synthesis of all of the types of reader-response dimensions as suggested by Beach, which we discussed in Section 6.2. Text World Theory is:

- **Textual:** in that there are explicit textual cues for the various types of world-building and shifts between worlds.
- **Experiential:** in that a key feature of the theory is that readers draw on schematic knowledge that is triggered by language and that this knowledge in all its forms (leant information, memories, experiences, emotions) plays a central role in reader's representations.
- **Psychological:** in that it draws explicitly on theoretical and empirical research in cognitive science and psychology.
- **Social and cultural:** in that it is sensitive to the contexts in which texts are read and the various external influences that shape readerly interpretations.

Text World Theory may be viewed as an example of cognitive *grammatics* (Halliday 2002), which we introduced in Chapter 1, providing a way for teachers to use linguistic knowledge as a tool to think with. Research by Giovanelli (2016, 2017) and Giovanelli and Mason (2015) has demonstrated how Text World Theory can be used to underpin the whole process of teaching literature in this way. For example, in Giovanelli and Mason (2015), we reported on a case study where a teacher had asked students to draw their initial impressions of the opening to a short story as a way of visually highlighting the kinds of schematic knowledge they were drawing on as well as which parts of the text appeared to be prominent and therefore significant. The teacher was then able to encourage students to think both about their own role in the reading process and strategically fed in contextual knowledge that the students could use to further develop their ideas. The teacher reported that she felt this was a good way of encouraging students to understand their roles as active participants in the literary transaction and to move away from relying on teacher-led responses.

Such a democratic approach to literature, which acknowledges the rich knowledge resources that students bring to the reading experience yet still highlights the role of the teacher as shaper, framer and introducer of new knowledge and ideas, may be a particularly useful approach with poetry, a genre that students can often find difficult, daunting and where they may simply want to defer to the authority of the teacher (see for example Snapper 2013; Xerri 2013; and within the parameters of Text World Theory, Giovanelli 2016, 2017). This kind of meta-reflective work can also support what Wolf and Barzillai (2009) call 'deep reading', a type of response exemplified by profound thought and a systematic engagement with a text on a personal level (see also Fisher et al. 2012 for discussion).

Our discussion above proposes a model of reading and of literary interpretation that rejects two extremes: first the idea that the meaning of the text simply equates to the author's intention;

second that the text becomes a practice in 'anything goes' with any one interpretation as valid as another. Text World Theory's emphasis on the principle of text-drivenness means that primacy is given to the language of the text itself; in other words, the validity of an interpretation can be judged by the extent to which it can be supported by language. For example, here is a poem by John Keats.

> This living hand, now warm and capable
> Of earnest grasping, would, if it were cold
> And in the icy silence of the tomb,
> So haunt thy days and chill thy dreaming nights
> That thou would wish thine own heart dry of blood
> So in my veins red life might stream again,
> And thou be conscience-calm'd–see here it is–
> I hold it towards you.

A brief Text World Theory analysis of this poem might begin by highlighting the shifts in world construction that takes place over the first few lines. The poem starts in the present, evident in the determiner 'This' and the adverb 'now', but moves via a conditional clause into a hypothetical world in which the speaking voice haunts the addressee of the poem: 'if it were cold'. There is a clear contrast in entities in the original and new text-worlds: 'living', 'warm' and 'capable' which initially described the 'hand' are now replaced by negatively-oriented counterparts 'cold', 'icy silence' and 'tomb'. The world-building and function-advancing propositions in this new world may evoke a feeling of coldness, of the absence of life and of a supernatural presence who, through a series of further shifts triggered by the modality of 'wish' and 'might' positions the reader further away from the opening of the poem and as a witness to a series of horrifying events. Finally, the adverb 'here' and the preposition 'towards' both of which encode proximity between the speaker and addressee mean that the poem ends (at least, to this pair of readers) in a dramatic and potentially immediate moment of terror.

Of course, we have no way of accessing John Keats' mind and consequently no way of definitively gauging what he meant in the poem. In this instance, appealing to some kind of authorial intention is pointless even if we may well have some mental construct of Keats in mind as we read (see Chapter 7 for more discussion of this). Equally, a response that ignores the language of the text is unlikely, we feel, to provide a satisfactory account of how the poem operates. A text-world analysis is thus well-placed both to ensure a tight focus on language and to encourage students to reflect on the kind of knowledge that they draw on when reading. For example, in our reading, 'icy silence of the tomb' is a particularly striking phrase, evoking a Gothic image of a cemetery, and a large stone tomb. This aspect (triggered by the language of the text) is fleshed out with knowledge of representations of hauntings and horror films and books we have read and through connections with other literary texts: both John Donne's 'The Apparition' and Shakespeare's *Macbeth* come to mind. For other readers, of course, different kinds of knowledge will be triggered and drawn on to construct meaning.

This final point also raises legitimate points about how much extra-textual knowledge is required, and how important this knowledge is relative to the language of the text. For example, we could have mentioned before we asked you to read the poem that 'This Living Hand' is largely believed to represent some of the final lines that Keats wrote before his death from tuberculosis at the age of twenty-five, that the poem was found in the margins of a satire – *The Cap and Bells* – and so may have been written as part of a larger work or intended for a future poem, that Keats was a Romantic poet, that he was greatly influenced by Shakespeare, Coleridge and Wordsworth. We could have provided you detailed descriptions of nineteenth century tombs and supernatural beliefs, of ideas about dreaming and imagination and their relationship to life and poetry, of Keats' illness and death (he actually died and was buried in Italy), of the poem's publishing history (it wasn't published until 1898, nearly 80 years after Keats' death). We could also have drawn on literary critical interpretations of the poem that variously argue that the 'you' of the poem is his lover Fanny Brawne and highlight the similarities between numerous poems of the time written to her by Keats, or claim that the poem is about the power of the Romantic imagination, or conversely that the 'you' of the poem is the modern reader who gives life to the poem through rereading. The list could go on ad infinitum.

If we conceptualise reading and studying literature as primarily about what we would call *knowledge-filling* then we would argue that this raises fundamental questions about the kinds of issues that we have been discussing throughout this book so far. It actually is perfectly possible to engage with 'This Living Hand' without much, if any, of the background knowledge we have just outlined – and indeed we would argue that a text-world analysis of the poem provides a clear and insightful analysis of the ways that the poem positions readers to adopt a particular perspective. We also think that teaching activities can draw on Text World Theory to enable students to consider the knowledge sources that they draw on in order to develop mental representations of their reading. This is not to completely dismiss the relevance of some carefully introduced extra-textual information to support and refine interpretations and to help develop more nuanced accounts of how literary texts fit into wider movements (see Giovanelli 2016, Giovanelli and Mason 2015 for discussion of this). We believe that these approaches can be useful when strategically used, but would argue against making extra-textual – and often niche – knowledge the way into teaching literature, or using this as the main criterion on which a student's understanding of a text is judged.

It also seems fair to say that the more extra-textual knowledge that is introduced, the more potential there is for students to move away from language of text itself and closer to what, in Chapter 2, we referred to as a 'manufactured' reading. Some of this extra-textual information may well be important and may be used – indeed GCSE and A-level specifications often highlight knowledge of different contexts as important, but we suggest that there is a danger in giving prominence to extra-textual knowledge that reduces literary texts to simple collections of historical or cultural facts. Instead, we would argue that knowledge of how language works is the first and most important step to understanding literature.

6.4.6 Text World Theory and classroom discourse

A final, and increasingly innovative, use of Text World Theory, is to support the analysis of classroom discourse to allow the teacher to explore the nature of interaction that students have as they discuss literary texts, which in turn can lead to decisions about teaching and learning strategies. For example, Giovanelli (2019) draws on the following taxonomy of types of group talk (Dawes et al. 1992; Mercer 1995):

- disputational talk, characterised by disagreement and lack of collaboration
- cumulative talk, characterised by uncritical agreement
- exploratory talk, characterised by critical engagement with others, constructive disagreement, and the sharing of alternative viewpoints which ultimately lead to a richer analysis

Viewing literature teaching as a dialogic discourse with the text and with others (see Eaglestone 2019) means valuing exploratory talk. In Text World Theory terms, such talk would usually include participants triggering shifts in world-structure through their use of negation, hypotheticals and modality which in turn place demands on other group participants in terms of how they track and respond. It also follows that explicitly encouraging or even teaching students how to engage in disputational talk, and by explicitly teaching them about the language that will enable them to do so could be beneficial as a discourse analytical tool. Text World Theory therefore has the potential to allow teachers to reflect on the interactions that take place in their classrooms (see also Ahmed 2019; Cushing 2019 for analysis of classroom discourse using Text World Theory in this way).

Activities and Reflections

1. Take a poem, or short episode from a novel, short story or play that you teach, and think about how you might use Text World Theory to plan out some activities. You could start by doing a text-worlds analysis yourself and see which particular language features are prominent and therefore worthy of attention in the classroom.

2. Use Text World Theory as a tool to encourage reflection on the kinds of knowledge that students bring to the reading event. For example, ask students to use sketches or short summaries to reflect on the different schemas they are drawing on as they read (see Giovanelli 2016, 2017 for examples of this).

3. Consider how and when you draw on extra-textual information and how this information is presented to students. For example, is lots of detail about Victorian England and biographical information on Dickens introduced at the beginning of Oliver Twist, before a student has had a chance to draw on their own knowledge, likely to be beneficial? Or, does this pre-figure certain responses to texts? What does the fetishisation of niche knowledge say about how literature and literary reading are conceptualised and the importance (or not) given to the reader? We have argued in this chapter that knowledge about language is more enabling for students. Would you agree? How does this fit in with examination requirements that students learn about contexts?

6.5 Disbelief, relevance and criticality

In Chapter 5, we outlined some research on immersion and discussed how readers who felt greater levels of transportation into the world of a narrative were more likely to have been affected by what they read. We shall return to these ideas for the remainder of this chapter.

Gerrig and Rapp (2004) explore *how* and *why* readers might be affected by reading fiction. Continuing with a metaphor of reading as form of travelling, in which the reader undergoes some kind of change, they argue that the extent of change will depend on 'the types of activities in which the traveller engages while on the journey' (2004: 267). Gerrig and Rapp rework the concept of the 'willing suspension of disbelief', which was originally coined by Samuel Taylor Coleridge. Coleridge posited that when readers pick up a book, they know that they are reading about fictional situations, events and characters but accept them as believable and consequently ignore improbable or unlikely scenarios. Gerrig and Rapp instead argue that the opposite is true:

when we read, readers accept the contents of a story unless they deliberately construct disbelief. In other words, readers need to *turn on* rather than *turn off* their critical faculties, consciously drawing on their knowledge and memories to take a more critical stance their reading. Gerrig and Rapp suggest that more reflective reading occurs when readers want, and are able, to put effort into disbelieving events and ideas: constructing disbelief is therefore a crucial part of developing a more critical response to literary works.

To illustrate their points, Gerrig and Rapp refer to an experiment that showed that readers are more likely to construct disbelief when what they read had strong personal relevance. In the experiment, the researchers gave groups of student participants two stories to read, one of which was set at their 'home university' and another which was set at an 'away university'. They then asked them to comment on the extent to which they agreed with a series of statements that were based on events in the story. They found that readers agreed more with the assertions in the story when they read the 'away' narrative, and were more critical of the statements when reading their 'home' narrative, drawing on various counter-arguments from memory in order to disagree with issues raised in the narrative. In other words, they more readily constructed disbelief when experiencing a narrative that had greater personal relevance. The experiment therefore suggests that personal relevance may be a key factor in supporting more critical reading. These findings are potentially interesting for the teacher in terms of considering the extent to which students are encouraged to take ownership of their reading and to draw on their own experiences and life resources when choosing texts to read. It also raises questions around how students are encouraged and enabled to respond critically to texts that appear to be outside of their immediate experience. We encourage you to think about these issues in our 'Activities and Reflections' below.

Activities and Reflections

1. How much attention is given to personal relevance in choosing books that students read in the classroom? Should teachers be more careful in devising tasks that consider the likely impact of making connections to students' lives?
2. If we take the points about personal relevance, the willing construction of disbelief and reflective reading seriously, should these be central concerns for the literature teacher?

Further reading

Overviews of reader-response theories can be found in Beach (1993) and Tompkins (1980). Stockwell (2020) contains discussion of more recent work from a cognitive linguistic perspective. Special recent editions of *English in Education* (see Giovanelli and Mason 2018b) and *Language and Literature* (see Whiteley and Canning 2017) on reader response have a number of useful papers. The first real attempt to undertake empirical reader response research in English was by I.A. Richards. Details of this work can be found in Richards (1929).

Louise Rosenblatt's work is remarkable and she seems to anticipate and influence many later theories and ideas about reading (including many that we have discussed and examined in this book). The best places to start are Rosenblatt (1978) and Rosenblatt (2005). Her influence on poetry teaching is immense; very good and useful examples of how teachers have worked with her ideas in the classroom can be found in Benton et al. (1988) and Karolides (1999). Long (2017) is an excellent recent discussion of work on personal response in the classroom.

The coverage we give to Text World Theory here is only partial, so if you are interested, do read more developed explanations of the theory. The original Text World Theory model is in Werth (1999), but updated, comprehensive yet accessible coverage is in Gavins (2007). Work focusing on Text World Theory within education includes Cushing (2018), Cushing and Giovanelli (2019), Giovanelli (2010, 2014, 2016, 2017, 2019) and Giovanelli and Mason (2015).

7
WRITERS

This chapter will:

- provide an overview of ideas about intentionality and the role of the writer in creating meanings;
- discuss intentionality, inferencing and mind-modelling from a cognitive linguistic perspective;
- explore how the writer is emphasised in different ways within English.

7.1 The writer and meaning

In the first part of Chapter 6, we provided an overview of some reader-response theories, including detailed discussions of transactional theory and Text World Theory. All of these reader-response theories posit a particular emphasis on the reader as a central element in the author–text–reader triad. In this chapter, we move the focus onto the author.

As we discussed in Chapter 6, literary and critical theories have placed varying degrees of importance on the author and their relationship to the meaning of a text. The move from more historical and biographical literary-critical work to New Criticism in the middle of the twentieth century reconfigured the emphasis from the author onto text. Then a further shift towards readers moved the spotlight again. At the moment, in literary studies at least, the degree to which the author remains a central or peripheral figure really depends on critical position adopted; it's perfectly possible to study literature through a biographical or a historical lens as well as through generic, textual and linguistic ones. As we saw in Chapter 6, all of these approaches, however, tend to marginalise the readerly aspect of the triad. In contrast, one of the strengths – and benefits – of a cognitive poetic approach exemplified in Text World Theory is that literary reading is viewed as a negotiated event between the writer and reader as co-participants in the discourse (this is also a key claim in Rosenblatt's transactional theory). The writer is responsible for providing directions in the form of language that act as cues to trigger aspects of a reader's knowledge, which in turn leads to the formation of rich mental representations. A text as such only comes into being as a result of this negotiation. Most readers are therefore aware, at least to some extent, of an authorial presence as they read. But what exactly is that presence and how can we understand the role of the author more precisely in the context of a reader-response model that we championed in Chapter 6?

In the remainder of this chapter, we argue that concepts and research from the fields of cognitive linguistics and cognitive poetics can answer these questions. In particular, we explore the presence of the author as an important mental construct that a reader has in mind when reading and consider the ways in which we can talk about an author's intention – questions that have troubled critics and educationalists for many years. We start by discussing some key ideas from literary theory around the middle of the twentieth-century that address the issue of intentionalism in the reading of literature.

In *Validity in Interpretation*, E.D Hirsch (1967) reacts against the New Critics' appeal to the centrality of the text and instead champions the author as the ultimate determiner of meaning. In the book's first chapter 'In Defense of the Author', Hirsch argues that understanding a literary work is simply a process of understanding what an author intended it to mean. Hirsch criticises the New Critical tradition's stance that words can in themselves convey meaning independently and therefore that the text can exist as an autonomous entity. Although Hirsch acknowledges the role of the reader in this process, his model, in contrast to Rosenblatt's transactional theory, foregrounds the author as the determiner of meaning.

Hirsch's arguments are complex and often circular, and his writing is not an easy read. One critical point he makes is centred on a distinction between 'meaning' and 'significance' (1967: 8). Hirsch argues that meaning has to be both an author-centred phenomenon and fixed, so that a reader's interpretation can only be considered accurate if it matches what the author meant (Hirsch later hedges this by admitting that we do not have access to an author's mind, but maintains we nonetheless should be able to work out what an author meant based on probability and looking at extra-textual sources). Hirsch also argues that although a reader may change their interpretation over time, this is merely a shift in what is viewed as significant and can always be measured against the text's original meaning. Hirsch thus frequently refers to 'validity' (1967: 3) as a measure of interpretations. He argues that a valid interpretation has to match what the author intended. The alternative, for Hirsch, is a kind of theoretical, practical and ideological chaos where 'no adequate principle exist[s] for judging the validity of an interpretation' (1967: 3). Such an approach, regardless of how we ever gauge what an author actually means, promotes a message that there is a definitive and recoverable answer to what a text means; in Hirsch's words, 'If a theorist wants to save the idea of validity, he has to save the author as well' (1967: 6).

Hirsch was reacting to a very influential essay, 'The intentional fallacy', by Wimsatt and Beardsley, who had vehemently argued against any possibility of knowing an author's intention. Wimsatt and Beardsley suggest that it is impossible to retrieve an author's intent even if that author is still alive, is available for questioning, or has otherwise given some indication of intentionality. As an example, they use T.S. Eliot's notes to *The Wasteland* which, although extensive, can never really reveal intention. They also compare what they term 'internal and external evidence for the meaning of a poem' (1946: 477). For them, internal evidence for meaning comes from the language of the text itself, which is retrievable to all, is public knowledge, and thus a good basis for thinking about meaning. In contrast, external evidence largely appears in material that is not part of the literary work itself; for example, biography, letters, journals, stories about what the author might have experienced, said or done that might act as a basis for interpretation. Wimsatt and Beardsley argue that appealing to external evidence, which lacks any real certainty, as opposed to the explicit language of the text, is a form of clairvoyance. In their final famous lines, they state 'Critical inquiries are not settled by consulting the oracle' (1946: cc).

This article and a later second one on the dangers of examining literature's emotional effects on readers (Wimsatt and Beardsley 1949) have influenced the ways that English has been conceptualised, taught and assessed both in schools and in universities (see also our discussion of emotions and literature in Chapter 8). Although Wimsatt and Beardsley are right to caution against the ascribing of intentionality, and probably provide a more convincing account of literary meaning than Hirsch, their essay is as problematic as his for two key reasons. First, their insistence on the centrality of the text downplays the reader just as much as Hirsch does; second, in positioning the writer as irrelevant, they dismiss the fact that readers often treat writers, and their intentions, as important. To address this second point, the next section examines ways in which cognitive approaches to literary study have examined how readers often construct a mental model of the author as they read. We consider the implications that this may have for reading and for studying fiction.

> **Activities and Reflections**
>
> 1. Hirsch's model of the author not only downplays the role of the reader, but also raises questions about the relationship between literary interpretations and knowledge. If we accept that the meaning of a text is solely equivalent to a retrievable author's intention, what implications does this have for how we teach literature?
> 2. Hirsch's more general ideas on knowledge have recently formed the basis for discussions around a 'knowledge-rich' curriculum (see for example Hirsch 2019). In Hirsch's terms, having one valid 'meaning' promotes a transmissive model of literary education where the teacher's role is simply to enable students to arrive at a particular and authoritative reading. How does this sit with some of the models of interpretation (e.g. Text World Theory) that we discussed in Chapter 6?
> 3. Can the meaning of a text simply be handed down as 'knowledge' from teacher to student?

7.2 Models of the writer

7.2.1 Real and implied authors

One way to disentangle some of the issues raised by Hirsch and by Wimsatt and Beardsley is to think about what we mean when we use the term 'author'. Generally, 'author' may be used to refer to two distinct roles: a person (the real flesh and blood individual) and a writer (the producer of a text).

This distinction appears in the work of Wayne Booth, who proposes differentiating the 'real author' (the flesh and blood individual) from the 'implied author' (the author relative to a *particular text* that the reader has in mind as they read). For example, reading *Great Expectations*, we can refer to the historical person Charles Dickens as the authorial figure (the real author). We have, however, no access to the real-life Dickens and have to rely on second hand extra-textual information, which will only ever be partial, to build up a mental representation of him. The implied author of *Great Expectations* is the representation of Dickens that we have in mind as we read that particular text; in this instance the implied author Charles Dickens is a different one to the implied author Charles Dickens of his early novels written some twenty years beforehand. And, of course, different readers may have different implied authors in mind based on their own knowledge and experiences.

Booth (1983: 71) terms these different implied authors 'versions', emphasising that these will change over time and over the course of an author's work:

> We must say various versions, for regardless of how sincere an author may try to be, his different works will imply different versions, different ideal combinations of norms. Just as one's personal letters imply different versions of oneself, depending on the differing relationships with each correspondent and the purpose of each letter, so the writer sets himself out with a different air depending on the needs of particular works.

Although Booth draws on the term 'second self' (1983: 71) to suggest that the shape of an implied author comes into being as a writer writes, an implied author is largely a readerly construct; that is, it is a version that is shaped by a reader's engagement with a text, and any extra-textual information available to hand. The reader in turn assigns intentionality to this implied authorial presence. We return to this important idea and how it has been challenged, adapted and used in recent cognitive linguistic approaches, in particular the work of David Herman and Peter Stockwell, in the next section of this chapter. First, there is one more element to add to the model.

Great Expectations is written by the real author Charles Dickens, understood by readers as the work of the novel's implied author, a version of Charles Dickens, but is narrated by the character and fictional entity Pip, who retrospectively tells his story to the readers. Pip's narrative voice thus represents a different level of telling to both the implied author and to other characters in the novel, who tell their own stories through the speech and perspectives that are assigned to them. There are, of course, different versions of the character of Pip as the novel progresses, from young child at the beginning to mature adult (see Chapter 8 for more discussion of this idea). The relationship between these different entities is shown in Figure 7.1.

Real author ⟶ Implied author ⟶ Narrator ⟶ Character

FIGURE 7.1 Fictional entities

7.2.2 A cognitive approach to intentionality

Booth's model and various subsequent variations have been influential in structuralist accounts of meaning, providing an interesting and useful distinction between the various roles and 'layers of telling' that exist in a narrative and the relationships between them. More recently, researchers working in cognitive linguistics and cognitive narratology have drawn on findings from psychology to re-examine how readers conceptualise and work with the notion of intentionality.

An interesting place to start is by looking at a very famous experiment that was undertaken in 1944 by Fritz Heider and Marianne Simmel. Heider and Simmel showed participants a short animation film containing a large triangle, a small triangle and a circle moving around the screen and in and out of a larger rectangular shape that had a door-like opening. Participants were then given some questions about the film and asked to explain their interpretation of what they had seen. The participants generally conceived the shapes as beings with motives for their actions and placed them as part of a larger narrative (for example, a number of participants said that the triangles were love rivals fighting over the circle). This study demonstrates that we tend to attribute mental states, motivations, personalities, and above all intentionality to individuals based on their actions (Figure 7.2).

David Herman (2013) draws on this powerful idea to propose his own model of what happens when readers engage with texts. Herman's work is grounded in research across various fields of

FIGURE 7.2 Screenshot from Heider and Simmel (1944)

psychology and linguistics, based on the premise that humans are 'intentional systems' (2013: 29), continually engaged in inferring reasons for others' behaviour across our everyday interpersonal practices. For example, if we see a friend start to cry and leave the room when watching television, we are likely to infer that they are upset and no longer feel able or want to continue to watch the programme. Herman argues that we also read narratives in this way; we are interested in what the text producer (in this case the author) has to say and their purpose for using language in a particular way. We draw on this simple desire to make sense of literary texts by making inferences and imputing intentionality onto the author as a co-discourse participant.

Herman argues that we naturally look for significance within narratives and that we use the language of the text to help us to do this. Rejecting the actual author/implied author distinction offered by Booth, which he suggests simply adds an unnecessary layer (we don't, after all, talk of implied speakers in face-to-face communication), he instead suggests that literary reading is simply a process of inference: we infer meanings in literary readings in the same way as we do for face-to-face communication – or any type of communication for that matter.

As we saw in Chapter 6, textual choices serve as cues for the construction of fictional worlds. Herman proposes that when we read, a writer's language choices lead us to infer that particular words, phrases or clauses are significant since they have been used over others. Engaging with fiction, like any other act of communication, is a process whereby we consider reasons for particular language and organisational features in a text, and then account for them as intentional choices.

To exemplify Herman's ideas, here is the opening of Ian McEwan's novel *Atonement*.

> The play – for which Briony had designed the posters, programmes and tickets, constructed the sales booth out of a folding screen tipped on its side, and lined the collection box in red crepe paper – was written by her in a two-day tempest of composition, causing her to miss breakfast and a lunch.
>
> (McEwan 2001: 3)

Following Herman's model, we begin by imputing to the author, Ian McEwan, the intention of describing a character (in this case Briony) to the readers, together with some information regarding what that character is like and what she has done. Here we also impute to McEwan the intention of wanting the reader to feel that this information is significant in some way. As McEwan uses the past tense, 'had designed', 'lined', 'was written', our inference here is that he intends the reader to picture the events being described as already completed. Similarly, the use of the word 'tempest' leads us to believe that McEwan intends us to view Briony's writing was frantic and probably messy rather than a calm, slow process over a period of time. And the fact that Briony missed breakfast and lunch encourages us to infer that McEwan wants to suggest something about Briony's character. This interpretation may well differ from reader to reader of course: one reader might read her as determined and focused; others might see view her as disorganised, and so on. Crucially, however, both these interpretations are driven by and grounded in the text.

This last point is important. Inferences may vary between readers (although variation is not infinite) and readers may return to those inferences, revising and refining as appropriate based on further knowledge gained from the text or through discussion with others, further reading and so on. Thus, interpretations are based on the best evidence available to a reader at a particular time and by consequence prone to being scrutinised, modified and rejected. Interpretations, in this respect, are also clearly never fixed.

Activities and Reflections

1. You can explore some of the ideas discussed by playing Heider and Simmel's film to students and asking them to comment on what they think is happening. Are there any patterns that emerge across a class or group of classes? How do groups of students develop and articulate a narrative based on the film? What kinds of resources and strategies are they using? What implications might these have for how literature gets introduced in lessons?

2. How far do you agree with the ideas put forward by Booth and Herman? Within the context of reading in classrooms, can you see any issues with what Herman, in particular, proposes about intentionality?

3. One of the ways that we can think about intention and how we use the term in literary reading is to consider revisions to work made by authors as deliberate intentional acts. Violeta Sotirova (2014) for example argues that any reworking of draft material must be evidence of intention (in making a change, an author intends to do something). How could you use this idea in your teaching to explore the idea of literary revisions? On place to start might be to look at Wilfred Owen's famous drafts of 'Anthem to Doomed Youth' available at the First World War poetry archive http://ww1lit.nsms.ox.ac.uk/ww1lit/

4. All of these ideas on intention can be used to encourage students to think about their own writing in terms of drafting, editing and so on. Encouraging students to think like authors offers a powerful way for them to better appreciate literary revisions. Can you think of ways that you might integrate the discussion in this section into teaching writing?

7.2.3 Mind-modelling

Peter Stockwell also draws on the human predisposition to find significance in actions, and to explain the motivation and intentions of others. Like Herman's ideas, Stockwell's concept of 'mind-modelling' (Stockwell 2009, 2016) is based on inferencing and treats literary reading as a communicative act in which readers impute intentionality behind linguistic choices onto writers. Within this model, the reader's conceptualisation of the author thus plays an important role in overall experience of reading a literary work.

Stockwell's ideas draw on the psychological notion of a 'Theory of Mind', the ability that humans have to take an 'intentional stance' (Dennett 1987) in relation to the actions of others so that we view these actions as a result of beliefs, emotions and feelings, which may well differ in certain situations to our own. This attribute is an important aspect of social cognition and usually develops between the ages of three and five in children. We draw on it in our everyday lives as we interact with others, infer reasons for their behaviour and position ourselves ethically to sympathise and empathise with them. Stockwell adopts the term 'mind-modelling' to take account of the creativity inherent in constructing a template of how a mind operates. We do not start from scratch when building up a model of a mind but instead use existing knowledge of ourselves and our interactions with others in the world in order to develop mental profiles. As well as engaging in this kind of work in our everyday interactions, we also model the minds of characters, authors and even other readers when we read.

Although often neglected in reader-response theories (Rosenblatt's transactional theory, for example, plays relatively little attention to the conceptualisation of the author, instead concentrating on the 'text' and the 'reader'), conceiving of real-life flesh and blood authors behind a text is an important way in which we engage with books. Of course, we understand an authorial presence as ultimately behind the various linguistic decisions behind writing and organising a text but we also often want to connect those texts to some aspect of the author's life, as though there is a direct point of access from the text to the author. As Stockwell points out, we can read or listen to television or radio interviews with authors (living and dead) and may even be able to meet them and engage with them at literary festivals, question and answer sessions, signings at book launches, and so on. In addition, we can also read autobiographies and biographies so that we build up a detailed mental model of that author's life, including connections with works written. This kind of information is often used by readers despite the fact that none of it provides access to an author's mind. It is unsurprising then that a consideration of what an author thinks or believes should be part of the experience of reading. As with any other communicative act, Stockwell argues, 'we assume intentionality and can then model a hypothetical intention [on the part of the author] on the basis of that presumption' (2016: 153). Although this modelling is similar to the ways in which we engage with the minds of real people, an important distinction is that with literary authors, such modelling is conducted solely through the medium of a literary text. Nonetheless, in the same way as we develop artificial or what Horton and Whohl (1956) term 'parasocial relationships' with characters in books, television programmes or films, we may also imagine such relationships with authorial figures.

Since modelling the mind of an author is a reader-driven and creative process, different readers will both typically vary in how they do so for a particular author and change their models over time. Readers also, in general terms, tend to converge in terms of what they think an author's intentions might be behind a particular work. Stockwell explains this by drawing on the notion of preferred and dispreferred responses, which originated in interactional sociolinguistics (see for example Pomerantz 1984). Although in the original sense the terms are used to explain expectations that exist within exchange sequences, for example a natural or preferred response to an invitation will generally be to either 'accept' or 'decline', Stockwell uses them in relation to readerly interpretations of a given literary work. Preferred responses to a text are those seem to be the most obviously natural and therefore acceptable based both on the language of the text and the kind of authorial mind that a reader has modelled.

We can return to Keats' poem, 'This Living Hand' which we discussed in Chapter 6 to exemplify this idea. The poem is a good one to use because readers generally interpret it in very similar ways; a very natural or preferred reading is to acknowledge this as a poem about the intensity of the speaking voice's feelings and emotions and as a nightmarish vision of horror. For example, here are some responses to the poem on the *John Keats Forum*, an online message board where users can post and discuss their interpretations of Keats' poems (http://www.john-keats.com/phpboard/index.php).

> **R1:** The deathly spectre of the hand of a dying man reaching out and 'earnest grasping' is a terrifying one, which is designed to frighten the reader.
> **R2:** I think he's talking about our desperate desire to keep a hold on our mortality – we'd rather kill someone than die, or at least let someone die in our place, even if we cared for them. There is also the secondary meaning that poetry, the symbolic work of the hands, can both resurrect the tormented poet and torment the reader to death, in the sense that they can feel his suffering.
> **R3:** I wouldn't like to be the person in receipt of such a verse!
> **R4:** He [the speaker] sounds very menacing.

All of these readers emphasise horror and strong emotions in their responses, a pattern that appears across almost every post. This then appears to be a preferred response to this poem and is captured in the kinds of comments R1–R4 make. In contrast, not one reader suggests that the poem is a happy one or that it evokes more positive emotions or is celebratory and so on, although it would be possible for this type of response to exist. To arrive at this latter interpretation, however, would clearly be a dispreferred (although not necessarily invalid) reading of the poem.

Of course, part of the experience of reading 'This Living Hand' resides in our knowledge that it was authored by the real-life John Keats. Although we have no access to Keats as we have previously discussed, we are able to model hypothetical intentions on the basis of knowledge about his life. Indeed, despite Keats being dead for 200 years, readers frequently and freely impute intentionality in this way. Here, for example, are three more responses from the *John Keats Forum*.

> **R5:** Do you think this was written for Fanny Brawne? I tend to think so, when K. [Keats] was at his lowest ebb and totally afraid of his life and what would become of it.
> **R6:** It [the poem] probably was written with Fanny Brawne in mind. The book I copied it from says that it was written 1819–20. A perspective of death from the living, where the living might feel the force of the dead, and perhaps feel a little guilty. Something like, you and me are equal, but you might hold the cup a little longer.
> **R7:** I've always presumed this to be directed at the critics who slammed Keats' work, particularly the writer of the Quarterly review of Endymion. I know that 'This Living Hand' was written a year later but maybe Keats was aware that his life was to be cut short by illness and so the poem was a bite back at the people who were so ruthless when it came to his work. I am sure that critics would not treat 'This Living Hand' the way they did 'Endymion.' In fact, I reckon that 'This Living Hand' had huge effects on earlier critics of his work. It is very chilling! Of course it's not about Fanny. It's about the people who tried so hard to make Keats' life a misery – the critics. Anybody else agree?

The readers here draw on a range of resources to support their modelling of Keats' mind, in the form of extra-textual knowledge about Keats, his life and associates as well as the general experience of different emotions (fear, love, anger). Comments like 'K. was at his lowest ebb and totally afraid of his life' (R5), 'with Fanny Brawne in mind' (R6), and 'Keats was aware that his life was to be cut short by illness' (R7) demonstrate both a specific example of mind-modelling in practice and how, for many readers, an integral and natural part of reading involves imputing intentionality to Keats as an authorial figure to generate a narrative behind the writing of this poem. More broadly such a practice occurs whenever we engage with a novel, story, poem or play and in doing so, aim to consider and articulate what we think the motivation behind that literary work might be.

> **Activities and Reflections**
>
> 1. One of the central premises of mind-modelling is that we do not start from scratch but build outwards drawing on the rich stores of knowledge that we hold about ourselves, others and the world. This means that personal idiosyncratic knowledge is important. Equally other types of knowledge would appear to be valuable for this kind of inferential work. How should this balance work when it comes to the study of literature? How do you view this in terms of the distinction that Wimsatt and Beardsley make between internal and external evidence?
>
> 2. You can explore the ideas of mind-modelling and preferred/dispreferred readings by choosing a favourite text of you own (and encouraging your students to do the same). How do you conceptualise the author? What might preferred and dispreferred readings of events and themes, characters, and the text as a whole be? You could also look at (or ask your students to research) responses to particular texts in online forums (*Goodreads*, blog posts and so on). What do these reveal?
>
> 3. The concept of preferred and dispreferred readings can be used to consider the age-old problem of how to account for unusual responses to texts. For example, it would be generally accepted that a reading of Owen's 'Dulce et Decorum Est' that viewed war in positive ways is a dispreferred reading. Are there some texts where we can positively discount certain interpretations? What implications does this have for how we teach those texts?

7.3 Working with models of the writer

7.3.1 Using the author as shorthand

In April 2019, the journalist Rebecca Reid appeared on the television show *Good Morning Britain* where she argued that studying the plays of Shakespeare was not the best use of students' time in the classroom, and that teachers should be drawing on material that was more relevant to young people. She announced her appearance on Twitter, where predictably, she received a wide and mixed set of responses. Interestingly, regardless of whether there was agreement with Reid or not, responses to both her television appearance and to her Twitter posts tended to be framed in a particular way. Individuals largely commented on understanding *Shakespeare*, liking or disliking *Shakespeare* rather than the plays themselves; in fact, there were very few mentions of specific plays by those who responded to her.

Using the name of an author as shorthand for their work can be explained through the cognitive linguistic notions of domain, metonymy and profiling. A domain, like a schema, is a general body of knowledge through which we understand a wider range of concepts. For example, we understand the months 'January', 'February', 'March' (and so on) against the wider knowledge domain of a calendar year so that using the word 'January' evokes not only the specific month but also the entire domain of a year. A year therefore acts as the conceptual background for the month that is explicitly stated (Langacker 2008); this is a particular kind of the figure-ground configuration that we discussed in Chapter 5.

Metaphor is a process of structuring one domain (a source domain) in terms of another (a target domain; see Lakoff and Johnson 1980 for the classic discussion). So, a phrase such as 'summer of my love', for example, would structure the abstract target domain 'love' in terms of the more concrete source domain 'summer', which would help us understand the former in terms of the latter (possibly warmth, passion and so on). Metonymy, in contrast, involves a 'shift in profile' (Langacker 2008: 69) within a single domain so that one aspect is used as a way of standing in for or representing another aspect of the same domain. So, the referent of 'Shakespeare' (as in the Rebecca Reid examples) is not the author himself, but rather his works.

Profile shifting by referring to the author to represent their works is a common way that we talk about books. For example, we might ask our friends 'Have you read the latest Stephen King?' or, in a bookshop enquire 'I'm looking for Margaret Atwood'. In both cases, the profile shifts from the usual referents of the proper nouns (the living flesh and blood authors) to a single book and a collection of their work respectively. A quick look at the bookshelves in one of our offices reveals titles on Shakespeare's plays called *Studying Shakespeare, Transforming Shakespeare, Novel Shakespeare* and *After Shakespeare*. Equally we talk of studying Shakespeare, watching Shakespeare, debating Shakespeare, liking or hating Shakespeare whilst all the time using the author's name as shorthand, through a shift in profiling, for his plays and performances.

These examples show how powerful the notion of an author actually is as a way of framing literature. They also suggest that the motivation for using metonymy in this way may result from our predisposition to impute agency and intentionality for their works onto authors. In essence, profile shifting satisfies the need we have to seek coherence by modelling a mind that is responsible for creating the stories we read. Gibbs et al. (1991) demonstrate this by showing that appealing to an authorial figure aids metaphor comprehension. In this study, the researchers examined the extent to which groups of participants drew on what they assumed to be the intentions of the author when analysing metaphors in poetry. They found that participants were more likely to consider metaphors as meaningful and arrive at a greater number of possible meanings when they were told that metaphors had been written by famous poets rather than generated at random from a computer. Flower (1987) similarly shows that when passages were difficult to comprehend or where meaning was ambiguous, readers tended to draw on the strategy of using knowledge about the author and from there impute intentionality onto the writer as a way of helping them to develop a response. In Section 7.3.2 we discuss some further implications of the author around teaching and assessment.

An interesting way that we can see how authors remain powerful in education can be seen in policy documentation that sets out lists of literary works for study by students in schools. For example, the National Curriculum for English programmes of study for reading have, from their earliest iterations, largely listed authors rather than their works. For example, here is part of a document for Key Stage 3 from 1995, the legacy of which remains today:

Pupils 11 to 14 – fiction by some of the following, at least two before 1900

R L Stevenson (Treasure Island), Mark Twain (Huckleberry Finn), L M Alcott (Little Women), Defoe (Robinson Crusoe), Hardy (Wessex Tales), C Bronte (Jane Eyre), Dickens (A Christmas Carol); Orwell, Stan Barstow, John Steinbeck, H G Wells, H E Bates, William Golding, J R R Tolkien, Nina Bawden, A Garner, L Garfield, R Sutcliffe, Ursula Le Guin, Penelope Lively, Jan Mark, Rukshana Smith, Michelle Magorian, Beverly Naidoo, Anne Holm, Berlie Doherty, Joan Lingard, Katherine Paterson, P Pearce, Rosa Guy, Marjorie Darke, Gwyn Thomas.

Poems – at least five of the following, including two pre-1900: Seamus Heaney, Ted Hughes, W H Auden, Eliot, Betjeman, Robert Graves, R S Thomas, D H Lawrence, Vernon Scannell, Siegfried Sassoon, Dylan Thomas, G Clarke, Robert Nichols, Elizabeth Jennings, Edwin Muir, Charles Causley, John Norris, James Berry, Cope, Stevenson, Blake, Coleridge, Hardy, Browning, Tennyson, Keats, Emily Dickinson.

Of course, the question of literary value has been framed through authors rather than works for a long time. For example, F.R. Leavis in *The Great Tradition* announced that 'except Jane Austen, George Eliot, James and Conrad, there are no novelists in English worth reading' (1948:1), and the then Conservative Education Secretary, Michael Gove, drew on similar sentiments of perceived authorial status to champion his claims for a return to a curriculum based on traditional values and canonical literature. In a speech to the school leaders' union ASCL in 2012, he praised the curriculum of a school where 'children study […] Jane Austen, Aldous Huxley and Primo Levi' (Gove 2012).

Finally, classrooms themselves become sites where authors may be enshrined and foregrounded as central to literary study. For example, Figures 7.3 and 7.4 show classroom displays that are focused on authors rather than texts or themes. Teachers are responsible for creating the

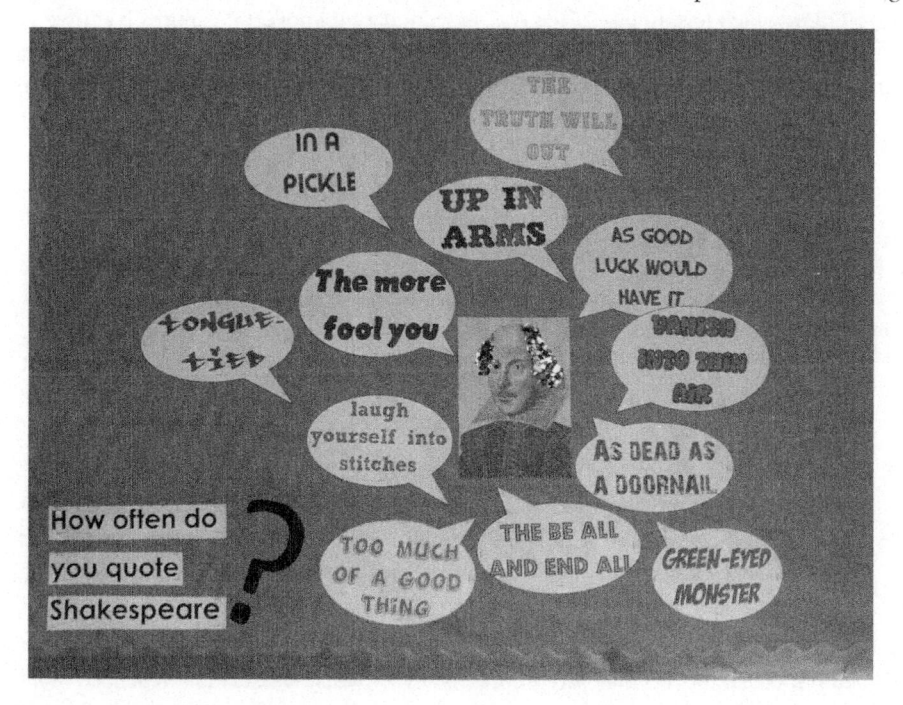

FIGURE 7.3 Shakespeare classroom display

92 Writers

FIGURE 7.4 Multiple authors classroom display

background in which lessons take place and, in secondary schools, this can involve the setting up of displays that in themselves act as powerful contexts, giving rise to ways of actualising the subject in relation to teaching and learning practices. Author-centred displays therefore give prominence to the role of the writer in literary study. For as Kress et al. (2005: 39) note, 'the displays

---

Activities and Reflections

1. How important is knowing about an author when studying a text? Some of the research discussed above has demonstrated the value readers place on knowledge of the author and our in-built strategy of looking for intentionality would suggest that the presence of the author in classroom discourse is important. If so, how does this fit with our discussion of readers in Chapter 6?

2. To what extent are young readers encouraged to draw on knowledge of the author in their personal reading outside of educational contexts? Are they encouraged to research authors as part of personal reading projects? To what extent do author visits, interviews, displays and so on form part of the extra-curricular life of the school?

3. Think about classroom displays that you have made or seen. Which aspects of an author or authors do they foreground, if any? In what ways should teachers frame authors and their works for students?

and arrangements of the classroom do not remain as 'inert', 'pre-created' background: they are activated, or reactivated, by classroom pedagogy'

7.3.2 Question setting

In terms of assessment, the author remains an important part of the way that the subject is conceptualised. For example, here are the four assessment objectives that relate to reading for GCSE English Language (as of June 2020):

> AO1: Identify and interpret explicit and implicit information and ideas select and synthesise evidence from different texts.
> AO2: Explain, comment on and analyse how writers use language and structure to achieve effects and influence readers, using relevant subject terminology to support their views.
> AO3: Compare writers' ideas and perspectives, as well as how these are conveyed, across two or more texts.
> AO4: Evaluate texts critically and support this with appropriate textual references.
> (DfE 2013a: 66)

As well as supporting examiners, assessment objectives are also used to shape teaching and learning practices in the classroom. Here, AO2 focuses on the writer's craft, while AO3 is more explicit in terms of asking students to construct a mind, complete with idea and viewpoints, and then to examine the texts that they are reading as evidence for this mind in operation.

The way that questions are worded in examination papers can also influence the ways that authors are conceptualised in teaching and learning activities. In current examination systems, questions are tightly controlled. In the two following examples, drawn from recent GCSE English Language papers, the impact of the assessment objectives discussed above can be seen on the questions that are set. In the first, the emphasis is very much on what the writer does; in the second, a more explicit attention to point of view is brought into focus.

1. How does the writer use language here to convey Mr Fisher's views on books and stories of the past?
   You could include the writer's choice of:
   - words and phrases
   - language features and techniques
   - sentence forms.
   (AQA 2018a: 4)

2. Compare how the writers convey their different perspectives on surfing. In your answer, you could:
   - compare their different perspectives on surfing
   - compare the methods the writers use to convey their perspectives
   - support your response with references to both texts.
   (AQA 2018b: 7)

Both these questions take an author-centred approach, foregrounding the role of the author and asking students to frame their answers accordingly. Both draw on vocabulary, 'choice' in the first and 'methods' in the second, that place an emphasis on craft and decision-making. The implication for teaching and learning more generally is that the author needs to be an integral part of studying English.

The examples above relate to GCSE English Language, but the same issues are pertinent to GCSE English Literature. Here, the assessment objectives are

> AO1: Read, understand and respond to texts. Students should be able to:
> maintain a critical style and develop an informed personal response
> use textual references, including quotations, to support and illustrate interpretations.
> AO2: Analyse the language, form and structure used by a writer to create meanings and effects, using relevant subject terminology where appropriate.
> AO3: Show understanding of the relationships between texts and the contexts in which they were written.
> AO4: Use a range of vocabulary and sentence structures for clarity, purpose and effect, with accurate spelling and punctuation.
>
> (DfE 2013b: 6)

Interestingly, for Literature, the assessment objectives have a dual emphasis on the writer as creator of meaning (AO3), and on the reader generating their own personal response (AO1). In examination questions, however, there is a single focus on the writer as shaper of meaning as the following example demonstrates – although perhaps here there is the implicit expectation that a personal response is valued.

> How far does Priestley present Eric as a character who changes his attitudes towards himself and others during the play? Write about:
>
> - what Eric says and does throughout the play
> - how far Priestley presents Eric as a character who changes his attitudes.
>
> (AQA 2018c: 4)

In general, examiners have three choices when putting together questions for papers:

1. questions that are author-centred; e.g. 'How does the *writer* present…?'
2. questions that are reader-centred; e.g. 'How do *you* respond to…?'
3. questions that are text-centred; e.g. 'How does the *text* convey…?'

Each of these represents a different way of conceptualising the reading experience for teachers and students. In the first, the question encourages the reader-student to focus on the writer's craft and most obviously encourages the mind-modelling of an authorial presence. In the second, the emphasis is on personal response. And in the third, it is the text element of the triad that is highlighted for scrutiny, much in the tradition of New Criticism. In this final type, the author and reader are more implicitly viewed as important.

The ways in which these question types get used across different assessments, as well as how assessments have changed across time, are interesting to explore. At the time of writing, questions that are author-centred are more prevalent across GCSE and A-level specifications in England, Wales and Northern Ireland; although looking back in time reveals that this was not always the case.

The following questions on Shakespeare's *Richard II* and *The Taming of the Shrew* are taken from and Associated Examining Board (AEB) A-level English paper from 1989.

1. EITHER (a) In what ways does Shakespeare present the conflict between the interests of the state and the interests of the individual in *Richard II*?

OR (b) Do you think that Shakespeare is offering hope for England in *Richard II*?

OR (c) "The relationships in *The Taming of the Shrew* are all flawed in some way." Do you agree?

OR (d) Can you take the ending of the play seriously?

(AEB 1989: 2)

These questions appear to be testing very different things (this was before the days of standardised assessment objectives), and each one encourages the student to work with the play they have studied in different ways. In (a) and (b), Shakespeare is explicitly mentioned; in (b) students are specifically asked to assign intentionality to the playwright. Arguably, in this instance it is the genre (history play) that frames the modelling of the authorial mind. The question invites a (new) historicist response that is rooted in the play's context of production and culturally-generated and performed ideologies (the nature of the monarchy, the deposition of a king, parallels between Richard and Elizabeth I, the authority and justification of Henry Bolingbroke, and so on). It does this, however, in a way that focuses on a strong authorial presence as the mediator of all of these concerns. In contrast, the questions on *The Taming of the Shrew* focus on the reader's response; in this instance (perhaps again this is an affordance of the genre), the questions' lack of focus on the author presumably mean that students could answer this question without commenting on the author at all. It is noticeable that these focuses on the personal and the affective have largely disappeared from assessments on literary texts within the secondary examination system.

The brief examples and discussion above raise some important questions more generally about the overall focuses of this chapter to which we now return. As we have seen, humans are predisposed towards taking an intentional stance to meaning (without which communication would be impossible) and the reading of literature can be viewed as an act of communication like any other. In this respect, authors are an important part of how we position ourselves in relation to and engage with works of fiction; for many readers, the author is a fundamental part of the whole experience of reading and thinking, speaking and writing about books. There are, however, some important differences between a prototypical face-to-face interaction and literary reading not least because authors and readers largely occupy a split discourse-world. As we have also discussed, we do not have direct access to an author's mind, and although texts are reasonable enough proxies of what an author might be thinking, they are never absolutes. In addition, as we have seen throughout this chapter the whole notion of authorship is conceptually and practically tricky.

We also know that readers are important as part of what Rosenblatt termed the 'literary transaction', although too often the emotional and affective aspects of literary reading, despite being important aspects of personal reading, can often be ignored in studying fiction within the school and assessment system. In contrast, they remain important in personal reading. In many respects, this is understandable given that examination questions are now required to be specifically rooted in assessment objectives to ensure consistency and fairness. It is easy to understand, therefore, how questions which do not focus on the personal are easier to set and more straightforward for awarding bodies and their examiners to assess. Perhaps, however, this is a system issue more than anything else.

Activities and Reflections

1. An interesting exercise would be to analyse examination questions that have been set across a particular set of years or on particular paper or from a particular awarding body. In what ways do questions emphasise one or more aspects of the writer–reader–text triad and what messages do these send about conceptualising the reading experience and for teaching?

2. What might be the best way of framing the writer–reader–text triad in classrooms and across assessment tasks more generally? One the one hand, authors are important and form part of the overall experience of reading; on the other, there are many caveats, as we have seen in this chapter, around attributing intentionality. Where can – and should – the balance lie?

Further reading

Hirsch (1967) is well worth reading to see the seeds of many of the arguments around knowledge and literary authority that exist in discourse about literature teaching in schools today. In Mason and Giovanelli (2017), we critique and challenge some of the assumptions made. The Wimsatt and Beardsley essays are useful reading; see Chapter 8 of Eaglestone (2018) for some good discussion of these and related ideas. Newton-De Molina (1976) is another classic text which contains both Wimsatt and Beardsley's 'The intentional fallacy' essay and several responses to it and to Hirsch's work.

The seminal work on the implied author is Booth (1983). Stockwell (2020) discusses this and related terms from a cognitive linguistic/poetic perspective. Herman (2013) is a thorough analysis of the process of modelling a mind through an inferencing that cuts out the need to have an implied author at all. Mind-modelling is first introduced in Stockwell (2009); the best single chapter in terms of both accessibility and examples is Stockwell (2016), and a good recent overview can be found in Stockwell (2020).

8
EMOTIONS

This chapter will:

- provide an overview of ideas about reading and emotion;
- discuss two cognitive models of characterisation;
- consider how engaging with characters can develop students' empathetic skills and promote social justice.

8.1 Why do we read?

This may seem like an obvious question, and perhaps the answer will differ depending whether we are arguing about an educational or a personal context. In this first part of the chapter, we take the stance that generally, in non-academic contexts, reading fiction largely results in people having strong feelings about a book and its themes and characters, and that a natural consequence of reading is engaging with and making sense both of our own emotions and those of characters that we encounter in texts.

In her critical survey of the parameters of literary studies as an academic discipline, Catherine Butler (2018) draws attention to one of the issues faced by undergraduate students of English (we would argue that this issue is the same for secondary students as well) when they commence their studies, namely whether the 'experience of literature itself' (2018: 12) in the form of personal response should be foregrounded as part of academic study. As Butler argues:

> Many people choose to study literature because they feel a deep intellectual and emotional commitment to the texts they have read. They expect that undergraduate study will involve learning to understand and express that commitment more effectively [...] Nevertheless they may find themselves warned by lecturers (and often by schoolteachers before that) to refrain from reporting on their personal experience of literary texts, especially in assessed work.

Butler suggests that there can be several unfortunate consequences of this viewpoint. First, it can result in students adopting an overly self-conscious academic register including clumsy use of terminology, where the way in which something is said (despite an appeal to objectivity) becomes more important than what is said. Second, a fear of responses being viewed as too subjective often results in students conjuring up 'in lieu of their own experience a mysterious figure known as "the reader"' (2018: 13). Since 'the reader' here, in the absence of any empirical study, really means the student herself, such terminology is little more than academic dressing-up (see also our discussion of readers and writers in Chapters 6 and 7).

Third, and possibly most importantly, the downplaying of personal experience is usually in contrast to an increased authority which is placed on the teacher or literary critic whose own readings become viewed as definitive. Often, the literary critic is given the ability of speaking for all readers. Butler, for example, discusses a passage in a poetry study guide by the notable critic Terry Eagleton which attributes a particular set of meanings to a Yeats poem. Here it is the critic's privileged status and authority that allows him to appear to offer an interpretation that would be satisfactory for all readers. As Butler (2018: 20) puts it, 'the very specific reactions, experiences, feelings and opinions attributed to "the reader" derive much of their rhetorical power from Eagleton's personal prestige as an eminent academic.'

Such practices may result in a disconnect between reading for pleasure and school education. In fact, we would argue that, in the classroom, the elevated status given to emblems of literary criticism such as the academic essay, and authoritative readings together with the devaluing of more personal responses arrived at through group talk and creative approaches may result in a particular vision of the subject. As David Miall (2007: 24) puts it: 'In our classrooms we may too persistently have called on students to marginalise their personal experience of literary texts to participate in the **game of interpretation**' (added emphasis).

One of the issues is that ordinary, non-academic reading is largely removed from the practice of literary criticism, upon which the study of fiction in schools is based. In an important study, Vipond and Hunt (1984), for example, found that readers were less interested in working out the meaning of John Updike's short story 'A & P', and more concerned with following matters of plot and character, and engaging with these in ways that were personal to them. Similarly, in a later study (Hunt and Vipond 1986), the authors found that readers were more attentive to evaluative rather than neutral narratorial comments, suggesting that aligning oneself personally with an implied author and/or narrator was a key concern of reading. A defining feature of literary reading is that it facilitates some kind of emotional connection either with a reader's own personal situation or else with the fictional events themselves. As Miall (2007: 36) puts it:

> The ordinary reader [...] is likely to stay close to the text itself, its character predicaments, plot turns and stylistic textures; her aim is to experience these rather than ask what the text might mean.

One problem that may arise from a disconnect between studying fiction in schools and more everyday reading practices is that students may be turned off English literature as a school subject. The tension between studying literature for enjoyment and for examinations is one that has existed for many years. Indeed, one hundred years ago, the 1921 Newbolt Report designed to provide a post-war review of and vision for education in schools in England, warned teachers not to

> [...] harp on the same method lesson after lesson, to read in class minute fragments of a whole which the class may well be relied on to read for themselves without assistance and at their leisure, to work in successive terms at one and the same book – all these make staleness in class and teacher inevitable.
>
> (Board of Education 1921: 112)

Arguably, the most recent round of reform in schools in England has accentuated this problem, although the picture is clearly a very complex one. The latest reforms to GCSE English specifications (from 2015) have included renewed attention on a narrow range of canonical texts, the marginalisation of popular and diverse fiction, and an emphasis on conservative literary-critical practices, including a fetishisation of metalanguage, and the removal of some popular fiction choices from GCSE specifications. These reforms may well be partly responsible for decreased enjoyment of the subject in school. As we write, uptake of English at post-16 is showing some small sign of recovery after decreasing at a steady and alarming rate over the last five years. This trend, whilst still affecting undergraduate numbers in English, suggests that students are being turned off literature, at least in a school context, between GCSE and post-16 study. Although at the time of writing, there has been no in-depth study of the reasons behind these numbers, some early research by the *English and Media Centre* suggests that a significant number of secondary English teachers have found that, in their own institutions, the content of the new GCSEs and associated teaching and assessment methods have not been well-received by students (see Bleiman 2017 for an overview).

Dissatisfaction with English at school brings with it a worrying cost, particularly given that numerous studies demonstrate the role reading fiction plays in supporting personal and social development (we return to this point later in the chapter) and in increasing overall attainment across a range of school subjects (see for example Clark and Rumbold 2006; Clark 2011; Sullivan and Brown 2015). *The Royal Society of Literature* (2017) IPSOS Mori public opinion poll on reading literature found that the benefits of reading are understood and shared by the general public. Research on shared reading groups by the charity *The Reader*, which examined the role of reading groups in mental health and other community (including educational) settings, found that reading literature can have significant life-long benefits, adding value to people's lives and helping them in times of trouble. Reading can also improve academic achievement, employability and wealth within a context of social justice and mobility: non-literature readers are likely to be male, from lower social backgrounds, have lower educational qualifications and/or aspirations (Davis et al. 2016).

Activities and Reflections

1. Should students use 'I' when writing about literature? What, for you (and your colleagues), are the advantages and disadvantages of this as a practice? You could think about current practice and guidelines in your own school, any advice you have read from awarding bodies, and your own experience as a student of English literature.

2. You might want to consider the extent to which academic (school) and personal reading should be aligned. This is a complex debate and different teachers will have different views. A useful starting point for looking at the impact of schooling on reading, as well as the *English and Media Centre* research that we quote above, would be the papers by Gary Snapper and Daniel Xerri that we reference in Chapter 5, both of which explore the degree to which students find the reading of poetry in school contexts difficult. Older papers such as Benton (1999, 2000) and Dymoke (2002) offer similarly interesting perspectives on the impact of assessment and education practices on teachers' and students' perspectives on poetry. Naylor and Woods (2012) also offer plenty of activities and points to consider on approaches to poetry teaching.

8.2 Feelings

Miall (2007: 53) defines a feeling as 'a subjective experience' that may appear in several forms including senses of liking or disliking a plotline, event or character and any range of immediate and sometimes unexplainable personal responses. Feelings are the engine room that drive interpretation and are largely responsible for schema accretion and refreshment (see our discussion in Chapter 2). In short, we depend on our initial feelings in order to respond to and inform meaning when we engage in reading.

Oatley (1994) argues that feelings arise from readers identifying with characters and events through a process of simulation. In this way, engaging with a book involves identifying with, and taking on, the various narrative actions and motivations that characters have. As Oatley (1994: 68–9) explains:

> When reading a novel or watching a drama we can take on a character's goals. We connect actions into meaningful sequences by entering them into the same planning processors. Then, remarkably, we experience emotions as these plans meet vicissitudes. The emotions do not just mirror those of the character. Though the plan is simulated, the emotions are our own.

Walton (1990: 214) suggests that although we understand fictional situations as not real, we develop 'quasi-feelings' about them. Like Oatley, he argues that fictional words provide the opportunity for playing out various scenarios and emotional responses in the relative safety of our imaginations. In addition, Walton suggests that the practice of reading enables us to project imaginative states of our own as we read so that our feelings and responses may include questions, anticipations and a whole range of immersive experiences (for example, see also our discussion on transportation in Chapter 5) that are guided by the words that the author has placed on the page. These ideas tie into the model of reading that we discussed in Chapter 6. In Text World Theory terms, mental representations are built up as textual triggers that project or invite a reader into a series of imaginative scenarios that are then fleshed out by the various kinds of background knowledge, experiences and stances that readers bring to a text with them. The reader's role in the experience of reading is therefore central and this experience relies on the response of a reader; reading, as we discussed, and as seen in Rosenblatt's terms, is a kind of transaction.

Oatley (2012) outlines a study that investigated the ways in which emotions guide interpretation. Participants completed pre-reading emotions ratings (the degree to which they felt happy, sad, angry or scared), read a short story, and then completed a post-reading emotions rating. The story was chosen because of its ambiguous ending, and participants were asked three questions that required them to provide some interpretative comment. The researchers found that those who felt sad after reading the story tended to state their interpretation first, and then move back through the story to provide evidence for their thoughts. Alternatively, those who felt angry after reading the story, worked their way through the evidence for their response first, before summarising it at the end. The researchers conclude that strong emotions can affect the ways that we respond to and explain our responses to fictional texts.

As well as being the primary vehicle for literary interpretation, feelings may also be important in broader terms. Miall (2007: 77–8), for example, argues that the ability to imagine and anticipate events and to engage with other entities and their feelings may have been important in the evolutionary context and thus facilitated survival. This could explain why we so easily have feelings evoked by a fictional text. Equally, the feelings evoked by unpleasant events in fiction (for example, horror, tragedy) may lead to further understanding both of our and others' fears and limitations. And the feelings that we have when we read may even mitigate loneliness (Hogan 2004) and promote physical well-being (Billington et al. 2010). Importantly, Miall (2007: 86) suggests that feelings can remain internal (what he calls 'first order'), but also give rise to a desire to shift our perspective on events outside of the text itself ('second order') so that we are primed and willing to change our behaviour to some extent and act on those feelings in a real-world context. It seems that reading fiction provides a unique forum for this kind of emotional work. We return to some of these ideas more in Section 8.5, but in short, feelings appear to support a personal growth view of English (see Chapters 2 and 7).

Pedagogically, a focus on feelings as a way into studying poetry was advocated by Benton et al. (1988) and through a series of later books that Michael Benton authored or edited. Benton's approach, typically involving questions designed to encourage personal response and engagement with the text, where a student's initial aesthetic experience with the text was considered of paramount importance (Benton was heavily influenced by Rosenblatt's transactional theory), offers a very different kind of literary pedagogy to one that emphasises background knowledge, authoritative interpretations and the promotion of metalanguage and a literary-critical academese.

Activities and Reflections

1. In Chapter 6, we argued against what we called 'knowledge-filling'; that is the offloading of information before the reading process begins. In Chapter 5, we discussed the idea of 'pre-figuring' which may result in particular ideas and interpretations being foregrounded for students. Both practices may downplay the student's experience with the text and may result in activities that are designed to re-present information back to the teacher. Considering our discussion in Section 8.2 and David Miall's comment that 'feeling drives interpretation', how can teachers build ideas about emotions into activities for students as they engage with texts?

2. Approaches like Michael Benton's were at the centre of literary pedagogies in English schools for many years although now appear to be marginalised (although see Bleiman 2020 for a call to renew the focus on a personal response to literature). Should 'feelings' rather than 'information' be at the centre of a literature pedagogy? What potential disadvantages (as well as advantages) might there be to this kind of approach? What do you think the gains might be? And what is in danger of being lost?

8.3 Modelling characters

In this section, we turn to how readers engage with the feelings of characters by outlining two cognitive theories of characterisation that we think are useful for the teacher. These theories are informed by ideas about how we construct, process and engage with fictional entities, highlighting that there are clear continuities between these practices and those that involve real people. Cognitive approaches thus differ from traditional 'literary' ones that emphasise the *difference* between fictional characters and real people, and define characters as sets of textual patterns with recognisable composite traits. These traits lead to a particular 'character' or groups of characters symbolising or representing some kind of overall thematic concern or concerns. So, for example, in *Macbeth*, Macbeth is read as a symbol of desire and ambition, and viewed as evil in contrast to Duncan and Macduff who are both good; Lady Macbeth represents guilt in the play, Malcolm stands for regeneration and hope, and so on.

Structuralist models of characterisation such as Propp's (1968) taxonomy of character roles based on Russian folk tales work in a similar way, as does E.M Forster's influential discussion of 'flat' and 'round' characters (Forster 1927). Forster distinguishes between those characters that are one-dimensional and symbolic (flat) and those which appear to be multi-dimensional and interesting (round). The latter category points towards a complexity that may be found in fictional characters in the same way as in real people (although Forster does not offer a convincing way of accounting for the flat/round distinction) and is in line with a more cognitive stance towards characterisation.

Cognitive approaches to characterisation, in contrast, emphasise the fact that we respond to characters in fictional texts and build up mental representations of them in the same way as we respond to people we meet in our 'real' lives. Cognitive approaches propose a similarity in the processing methods that we use in each context and view fictional characters as constructs of the human mind influenced by textual detail, but crucially developed through our own background knowledge and imaginative capabilities. Jonathan Culpeper's model for 'comprehending character' (Culpeper 2001: 35) provides a good example of such an approach. Culpeper proposes that reading involves a combination of 'top down' and 'bottom up' processes whereby details from the text combine with schematic knowledge to create representations (in this way Culpeper's model works within the same parameters as Text World Theory). So, readers assume a particular stance (reading for character) which acts as a 'control system', guiding the kinds of knowledge that will be seen as useful for the understanding of character. This knowledge is used to flesh out information processed from the text and provide representations (our sense of character) in the 'situation model', but crucially, the text itself also regulates the type of knowledge that is likely to be useful (this equates to Text World Theory's notion of text-drivenness) so that the process does not become overloaded.

The model we draw on for the remainder of this section is Stockwell's account of mind-modelling, which we first introduced in Chapter 7. As we discussed in that chapter, mind-modelling involves making inferences about others' psychological states and then constructing a model of their mind. The model is informed both by interactions with them, and by more general mental templates of human behaviour. As Stockwell (2020: 177–78) argues:

> The key to understanding a fictional character is understanding what a person is. In your own mind, you have the prototypically best example of a person – and it is you. In the most basic sense, you know what it means and feels to have a conscious awareness, and subconscious thoughts, moods and inclinations. You know what emotions feel like and the sorts of things that cause them. You know what it is to inhabit a human body and a life in this world and interact with other people, and exist in a social community.

Stockwell views mind-modelling as an active process where a reader adopts a role of 'taking textual cues and shaping them into a person' (2020: 179). The degree to which this process results in a rich sense of character relies both on the investment a reader wishes to put in to the reading experience, and on the text itself; put simply, a reader has to be engaged and motivated to read, and the text needs to be of a quality that it provides suggestive material for a reader to act on. In the latter respect, Stockwell (2020: 179) suggests that texts that have the following textual patterns are likely to lead to a richer sense of character developing:

- direct descriptions of appearance and manner;
- instances of direct speech to suggest character autonomy or thought so as to give the reader access to a character's mind;
- the thoughts and reactions of other characters which provide complementary or alternative viewpoints on a particular character to our own.

As an example of how these textual elements might work, here is a famous extract from the opening of Charles Dickens' *Great Expectations*, a text which regularly appears on GCSE and A-level specifications.

> Ours was the marsh country, down by the river, within, as the river wound, twenty miles of the sea. My first most vivid and broad impression of the identity of things seems to me to have been gained on a memorable raw afternoon towards evening. At such a time I found out for certain that this bleak place overgrown with nettles was the churchyard; and that Philip Pirrip, late of this parish, and also Georgiana wife of the above, were dead and buried; and that Alexander, Bartholomew, Abraham, Tobias, and Roger, infant children of the aforesaid, were also dead and buried; and that the dark flat wilderness beyond the churchyard, intersected with dikes and mounds and gates, with scattered cattle feeding on it, was the marshes; and that the low leaden line beyond was the river; and that the distant savage lair from which the wind was rushing was the sea; and that the small bundle of shivers growing afraid of it all and beginning to cry, was Pip.
>
> 'Hold your noise!' cried a terrible voice, as a man started up from among the graves at the side of the church porch. 'Keep still, you little devil, or I'll cut your throat!'
>
> A fearful man, all in coarse gray, with a great iron on his leg. A man with no hat, and with broken shoes, and with an old rag tied round his head. A man who had been soaked in water, and smothered in mud, and lamed by stones, and cut by flints, and stung by nettles, and torn by briars; who limped, and shivered, and glared, and growled; and whose teeth chattered in his head as he seized me by the chin.
>
> 'Oh! Don't cut my throat, sir,' I pleaded in terror. 'Pray don't do it, sir.'
>
> (Dickens 1861: 3)

In this extract, the narrator Pip is recounting an incident from his childhood when he first met the convict Magwitch. The account of the physical surroundings and family history provides rich detail for the reader to model Pip's mind and perspective both as child and as adult reflecting on that experience, 'the small bundle of shivers growing afraid of it all and beginning to cry'. The account also provides detailed description of Magwitch so that the reader is able to develop a rich sense of the convict and his character in the space of only a few lines. Pip's description of Magwitch begins with direct speech, dramatically breaking the long narrative which precedes it; the surprise nature of Magwitch's words is accompanied by a description of his sudden appearance, he 'started up from among the graves'. Magwitch's words, threatening violent action towards the young Pip, project a dangerous mind and character, a point evident in Pip's framing reporting clause 'cried a terrible voice'. When Pip begins to describe Magwitch, he does so in a way that provides further direct narratorial description, inviting further fleshing out of both characters. He starts with an adjective 'fearful' and then a precise description that cumulatively invites the reader to build up a picture of Magwitch's physical state and model his mind: his impoverished physical state and lack of clothing; his physical suffering; and the danger he poses to Pip through his own violent actions. A striking stylistic pattern is the shift from passive forms 'a man who had been soaked in water, and smothered in mud, and lamed by stones' to active ones, 'who limped, and shivered, and glared, and growled […] as he seized me by the chin.' All of this projects a character who is first presented as a sufferer and then as an active threat to Pip.

Overall, the movement of the passage follows Pip's own thought process as he views Magwitch first as a frightening sight and then a risk to his own safety. This latter point is supported by the direct speech that follows in which Pip's pleas to Magwitch are again given specific framing, 'I pleaded in terror', so as to emphasise his own mind at this time. Dickens' first-person narrative thus allows the reader to mind-model Pip (and begin a process of mind-modelling which continues throughout the novel). In addition, and crucially, Pip's narration, thought and direct speech also provide the basis for the mind-modelling of Magwitch. The effect in this passage is therefore of rich characterisation in which two distinctive minds are modelled: Pip the child and Magwitch the dangerous criminal.

It is important to remember that the mind-modelling of characters will vary from reader to reader. The central premise of all cognitive approaches to characterisation is that a combination of text-based cues and reader knowledge are responsible for building up characters, and this means that we can never talk of a single 'character' but must instead recognise that different readers will necessarily generate their own versions of characters that, in turn, will be prone to further refinement through re-reading, reflection and talking to others. Of course, the constraints of the text will narrow down the possibilities: it would be unlikely, for instance, that readers would mind-model Magwitch as presented in the passage above as a kind and gentle man. And, readers may be influenced by representations in different modalities. For example, there are multiple film and audiobook versions of *Great Expectations*, and teachers often use these as learning materials which can influence the ways in which students later respond to the characters when reading the novel: you could look, for example, at the ways in which Pip and Magwitch are presented by the camera at the opening of one or more film versions. Nuances in the ways that readers mind-model, and, from a classroom perspective, how students are encouraged to reflect on that process, provide interesting opportunities for the teacher to explore.

Activities and Reflections

1. A 'character study' is a popular teaching activity, as well as being a frequent focus of examination questions at GCSE and A-level. Given our discussion in this chapter about the process of characterisation and how readers draw on their own knowledge and sense of what a 'person is', how might such studies be set up to take account of differences in the ways that readers mind-model and consequently the mental constructs of characters that they build and might want to talk about in their responses to literature? A good starting point might be to look at examiners' marking schemes to see the extent to which these recognise the dynamic and often idiosyncratic act of mind-modelling. Is there flexibility in marking schemes for acknowledging that mind-models of characters will be different from reader to reader, or do they appear to reward singular ways of responding to characters in literature?

2. Stockwell's list of textual patterns above suggests that the quality of text is important: some texts will inevitably lead to richer types of mind-modelling than others. This clearly has implications from a teaching perspective but what exactly does this mean? What qualities should a text have (beyond linguistic ones)? Is there room here to argue for the ability for a text to engage and be relevant to its readers as important attributes to facilitate mind-modelling, and therefore lead to more fruitful teaching opportunities?

8.4 Characters, enactors and selves

In our discussion of Text World Theory in Chapter 6, we outlined that characters were important world-building elements that help us to form and then build up mental representations as we read a literary text. Text World Theory recognises that our representations of characters throughout the reading process are dynamic in so far as we are asked to track different versions of a character as they are presented to us over time. In fact, as a result of this, current versions of Text World Theory adopt the term 'enactor' (Gavins 2007: 41) rather than 'character' to account for the different conceptualisations that we face when tracking fictional entities in a text. We can redefine the various representations of a fictional entity as 'enactors' of that entity and 'character' as the more holistic and overall impression gained from tracking and experiencing those enactors over the course of reading.

A good example of how this works can be seen in *Great Expectations*. At the opening of the novel, we are presented with an adult Pip whose narration takes us back to imagine a younger Pip. Over the course of the novel, we engage with other versions or enactors of Pip: the Pip that first meets with Miss Havisham and Estella; the Pip that moves to London; the Pip that meets Magwitch again; the Pip that moves to Egypt, and so on. Of course, the novel helps us to handle all these mental representations so that we understand them as versions of the same entity, and this allows us to conceptualise Pip as a character across the novel as a whole; each updated enactor results in a kind of super version that gives rise to a certain way of thinking about a novel's character as a whole, called a 'composite enactor' (Giovanelli 2013: 102).

Of course, a reader can also become an enactor and the degree to which readers feel immersed in stories is important, as we discuss in Chapter 5, in considering the value of the reading experience. There are some key textual features that facilitate this kind of reader positioning. For example, the use of the first-person is an invitation to the reader to take on the role of a narrator or character-enactor. The extent to which this comes about will depend on a number of factors such as the content and reliability of the narrating 'I', the values they appear to hold as a character, and the reader's disposition and willingness to align themselves with the speaking voice. Eccentric and/or unreliable narrators such as in Poe's 'The Tell-Tale Heart' and narrators who have unfavourable characteristics such as in Browning's 'My Last Duchess' and 'Porpyhria's Lover' may be kept at a distance. Competing and conflicting narrative centres, for example in Shelley's *Frankenstein*, may make it difficult for us to align ourselves fully to one narrating voice or else demand that we re-evaluate our position following an alternative perspective on narrative events.

The use of the second person pronoun 'you' may invite a different kind of immersive experience, known in Text World Theory as 'self-implication' (Gavins 2007: 87). There are several ways in which a reader might understand 'you' when reading. Three important ones are:

1. **Generic 'you', referring to a broad, unspecified audience** e.g. 'You could pick it up by the loose flap of a roof/and all the houses would come up together/in the same pattern attached, inseparable' in Patricia Goedicke's 'You Could Pick It Up'.
2. **'You' referring to a fictional character in a text** e.g 'Since none puts by/The curtain I have drawn for you, but I' from 'My Last Duchess' where the 'you' here is the visitor being taken on tour by the Duke.
3. **'You' referring outwards explicitly to the reader** e.g. 'If in some smothering dreams, you too could pace/Behind the wagon that we flung him in', from Wilfred Owen's 'Dulce et Decorum Est'.

Sometimes 'you' may be directed both to a character within a text and to the reader outside it, a phenomenon known as 'double-deixis' (Herman 1994).

Of course, the degree to which a reader will self-implicate and identify themselves as the 'you' of the narrative will depend, just as with the use of the first-person, on a number of factors. It may be, however, that the extensive use of 'you' in a text gives rise to certain effects, and these are worth exploring with students. Of equal interest are those texts which use both the first and second person. Here, for example, is Thomas Hardy's 'Neutral Tones', which appears in AQA's GCSE English Literature Poetry Anthology, a poem which relies on an interaction of pronouns: both 'I' and 'you', and then the collective 'we'.

> We stood by a pond that winter day,
> And the sun was white, as though chidden of God,
> And a few leaves lay on the starving sod;
> – They had fallen from an ash, and were gray.
>
> Your eyes on me were as eyes that rove
> Over tedious riddles of years ago;
> And some words played between us to and fro
> On which lost the more by our love.
>
> The smile on your mouth was the deadest thing
> Alive enough to have strength to die;
> And a grin of bitterness swept thereby
> Like an ominous bird a-wing…
>
> Since then, keen lessons that love deceives,
> And wrings with wrong, have shaped to me
> Your face, and the God curst sun, and a tree,
> And a pond edged with grayish leaves.

The poem starts with 'we', an invitation to position ourselves as an enactor in the main text-world either as the addresser or addressee. The poem appears to invite the reader to move between these two positions: this is maintained in the second stanza with the use of a second person form, 'Your eyes', and then two collectives 'us', and 'our'. The phrases 'your mouth' (third stanza) and 'Your face' (fourth stanza) make a strong appeal to the reader to identify with the 'you' of the poem.

At the same time, the use of the first-person, 'we' and 'me', invites the reader to take on the speaking voice. The poem's content, with its emphasis on sadness and the end of a relationship and its images of loss and decay, provides a particularly poignant context, and it may also be that readers are influenced by their own life experiences or even initial responses as they align with either addresser or addressee.

It is worth pointing out that some readers may, of course, struggle to self-implicate at all. In Hardy's poem, the experiences and feelings of the enactors may be far removed from the reader's, and even the language of the text may not help to facilitate a sense of alignment.

Activities and Reflections

1. High self-implication when reading is an important part of developing empathy. We discuss some of the issues and implication around character and empathy in the next section, but for now, what kinds of approaches might be needed to teach literary texts that ask readers to represent enactors of themselves in different ways? You could use the difference in 'you' between 'My Last Duchess' (textual 'you') and 'Dulce et Decorum Est' (reader 'you') as a starting point.
2. Following our discussion of 'Neutral Tones', what implications does the fact that some readers may struggle to self-implicate have for teaching? Is a rich understanding of some literary texts difficult if students cannot access ideas and emotions within them? What can and should teachers do about this?

8.5 Empathy and social justice

So far in this chapter we have explored the ways in which reading fiction is driven by the feelings that are cued up when we immerse ourselves in a reading experience. We have also considered the ways in which we engage and align ourselves with the various enactors of characters and ourselves that exist in the rich mental representations of fictional worlds that are formed as we read. We now turn to some wider implications of these processes and consider literary reading in a more applied sense. In other words, we think about the value of reading in the outside world and what this might mean for the ways we understand and frame studying fiction in schools.

For many years, one argument for the centrality of literature in the English curriculum has focused on its humanising qualities and its ability to facilitate readers' moral and spiritual development. For example, the influential post-First World War Newbolt Report had argued that literature teaching introduces students to a 'greater intellect' and 'contact with great minds' (Board of Education 1921: 15) and was 'a record of human experience' (1921: 11), which 'tell[s] us what all men are like in all countries in all times' (1921: 205). These ideas were most famously taken up by F.R. Leavis (Leavis had studied under a member of the Newbolt Report committee) and developed into theories and practices of English teaching that broadly align with Cox's 'cultural heritage' model of English, a need to define the subject in terms of a journey through key canonical texts that together constitute the best work of a culture and society. As we explored in Chapters 4 and 7, these views can often give rise to hierarchies of authors and their texts, with certain kinds of genres being elevated and championed and others being marginalised and or dismissed. This view has underpinned pedagogies of literary reading that have emerged in England following the election of the Conservative-Liberal Democrat coalition government's education reforms in 2010. These include the fetishisation of background knowledge and its emphasis in pedagogy, and a model of teaching where information about texts is transmitted (or directly instructed) from teacher to student. We have commented on these issues in earlier chapters of this book.

An alternative way of thinking about literature moves away from focusing on institutions, canonical texts and the transmission of knowledge, and instead recognises the social (both personal and interpersonal) power of reading. Human life, after all, is social life: we work, live and breathe in communities (both physical and virtual), and use language to direct others' attention to ideas we want to express, giving them cues to construct mental representations of our words so they can communicate back to us. As we have seen in this chapter, we engage with fictional characters, largely drawing on the same processes as we do to engage with real people. In fact, the modelling of others' minds is a ubiquitous phenomenon. We infer people's thoughts, feelings and motivations intuitively and use these to guide our interactions with them. The relationship between modelling the minds of fictional and real people is a bidirectional one; we draw on our real-life processes to help us navigate fictional worlds, but our experiences with literature also feed back into our everyday actions. In simple terms, this means that literature really does have transformational power: Fiction helps us improve our mental models, which may sometimes be partial or wrong, and may help us to understand events and people in our lives and lead to behavioural changes.

In a study of parents' shared reading with four to five-year-old children at home, Adrian et al. (2005) examined this phenomenon, exploring the relationship between frequency of reading and the degree to which parents encouraged their children to consider the mental states of characters in books. The researchers found that children were better at mentalising (thinking about and discussing what people might think) if they were read to more frequently and if their parents made suggestions about the minds of characters as they read. In other words, engaging with and discussing fictional characters' minds on a regular basis provided the children with a template for inferring the mental states of real people. This supports research more widely which suggests that a lifetime reading habit improves the ability to mentalise (Mar et al. 2006; Kidd and Castano 2017).

According to Janet Alsup (2015), this modelling of the mental states of others that occurs when we read gives rise to a series of processes whereby behaviour changes as a result. In Alsup's model, shown in Figure 8.1, emotional, behavioural and attitudinal changes occur as a reader engages with a text. This is first a result of a process of *identification* as a reader draws on real-world knowledge to make connections between the world depicted in the text and the real world. This identification creates *empathy* which guides the reader within the text, but also beyond it, so that they align themselves more fully with events and characters in the text. Finally, *social action* extends the influence from the text to the real world completely, providing a larger context for the reading experience and effecting some sense of change in the reader. This final change may be highly personal, for example giving rise to reflection on a personal situation or experience, or affecting the reader's ideological position

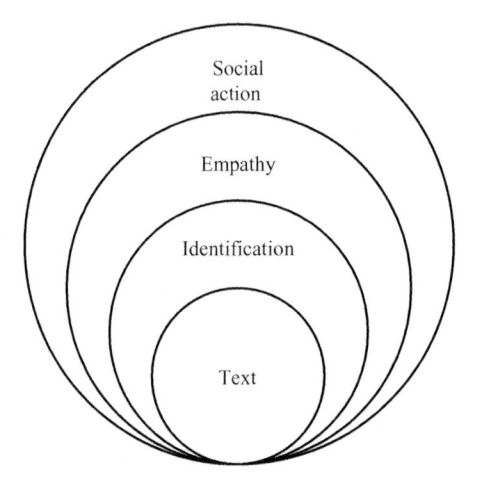

FIGURE 8.1 How reading changes behaviour (from Alsup 2015: 71).

in some way, or even grander and more dramatic such as prompting some explicit social action that helps others. A study that supports Alsup's theoretical model is Lee et al. (2014), who found that young children's behaviour was positively affected by stories that promoted the benefits of being good. Similarly, Johnson (2012) asked adult readers to read a short story and, when they had finished, to indicate the degree to which they felt transported (see our discussion in Chapter 5). Those readers who reported being more transported showed higher levels of empathy for the characters in the story but crucially were also more likely to engage in helpful behaviour towards others after reading. And, Vezzali et al. (2015), found that reading *Harry Potter* resulted in improved attitudes among readers towards minority and stigmatised groups. It seems therefore that reading literature can literally make you a better person; as Johnson (2012: 154) suggests 'reading narrative fiction allows one to learn about our social world and as a result fosters empathic growth and prosocial behaviour'.

Activities and Reflections

1. How can literature be used to facilitate social action and social justice? Does this depend on the texts chosen by the teacher, by the teaching approach, or by both? Consider the books that you currently teach in your department: in what ways might they enable the kind of staged process described by Alsup (Figure 8.1)? Are the ways in which they are taught focused on moving outside of the text to consider wider societal issues? Are students encouraged to take their reading further once their study has been completed?

2. Read the online lesson plan to Claudia Rankine's poem 'From Citizen, VI [On the train the woman standing]', taken from *Citizen: An American Lyric*, a collection which explores various forms of racism. The activities are centred around a number of objectives, including to lead students 'into reasoned discussion about ways to make all members of the American community equal, not only in the eyes of the law, but in the eyes of one another'. What do you think of the activities and approach in the light of our discussion in this chapter?

    https://poets.org/lesson-plan/incredible-bridges-citizen-vi-train-woman-standing-claudia-rankinee

Further reading

Webb (2019) focuses on students as critics and writers, and proposes ways that they can develop an academic mindset without simply repackaging pre-taught ideas. Miall (2007) offers an extensive overview of the relationship between feelings and literature in a very accessible set of chapters. Oatley (2012) is a similarly good overview of how emotions guide the reading of fiction. Suggestions for Stockwell's work on mind-modelling were provided at the end of Chapter 7. For a paper specifically on characters in fiction (Charles Dickens), see Stockwell and Mahlberg (2015). Giovanelli (2017) uses Text World Theory to explore how students draw on background knowledge to mind-model characters in poetry and how they reflect on this process. Mar (2018) is a thorough account of current research on reading and social cognition. Alsup (2015) is a superb overview of the value of reading literature in schools in the context of empathy and social action and contains ideas for the classroom at the end of each chapter.

CODA

Our discussion in this book leads naturally, we feel, to a short series of statements that we offer here as a final set of reflections both to teachers and to researchers. We hope that you will continue, in the spirit of this book, to think about and discuss these statements in the light of your own context and experience.

1. English in schools has a long history of contestation and debate, including around the study of fiction and the curriculum.
2. Reading in schools is complex due to the various constraints of politics, policies, and external and internal accountability.
3. Cognitive linguistics and cognitive poetics offer ways of reconceptualising issues and reconfiguring the ways in which we consider and talk about reading in education. These models can help us understand how we mentally engage with texts, authors and other readers, and can give teachers fresh insights into curriculum and assessment matters.
4. Text choices are never neutral but are informed by ideological and practical concerns. Hierarchies and prejudices exist towards certain texts which may be unhelpful.
5. What readers bring to a reading experience is important, both in terms of their knowledge and their personal and status-driven identities.
6. The extent to which we give prominence to the author, to the reader and to the text matter and can reveal fundamental ideas about how we value studying fiction.
7. Studying fiction in schools may be disconnected from other reading practices. Some of this is inevitable but other issues could be re-examined given what we know about what motivates readers in non-academic contexts.
8. The personal and emotional aspects of reading are often neglected in education spaces. This may be because of assessment and other constraints, or because these aspects are seen as unimportant and/or not academic. The emotions, and reflections on pro-social behaviours, that may arise as a result of a focus on these aspects are important in considering the connections between studying fiction and social justice and action.

Taken together, these statements present a set of premises that we think can provide a starting point for reconfiguring the ways that we conceptualise the study of fiction in schools. We believe that advances in cognitive poetics, both now and in the future, will help us to understand what it means to engage with fictional characters and worlds and, ultimately, to improve the experience of reading for young people in our classrooms.

REFERENCES

Adrian, J. E., Clemente, R. A., Villanueva, L., and Rieffe, C. (2005) 'Parent–child picture-book reading, mothers' mental state language and children's theory of mind', *Journal of Child Language* 32: 673–86.
AEB (1989) *General Certificate of Education Advanced Level English Paper 2*.
Ahmed, F. (2019) *An Exploration of Students' Construction of Knowledges and Identities During the Reading of Literature using Text World Theory*, Unpublished PhD Thesis, Aston University.
Allington, D. (2011) 'Distinction, intentions and the consumption of fiction: Negotiating cultural legitimacy in a gay reading group', *European Journal of Cultural Studies* 14(2): 129–45.
Allington, D. (2012) 'Private experience, textual analysis, and institutional authority: The discursive practice of critical interpretation and its enactment in literary training', *Language and Literature* 21(2): 211–25.
Alsup, J. (2015) *A Case for Teaching Literature in the Secondary School*, New York, NY: Routledge.
Anthony, L. (2014) AntConc (Version 3.4.1w) (Windows). Tokyo, Japan: Waseda University. Available from http://www.laurenceanthony.net/
Appleyard, J. A. (1990) *Becoming a Reader: The Experience of Fiction from Childhood to Adulthood*, New York, NY: Cambridge University Press.
AQA (2018a) *GCSE English Language Paper 1*, https://filestore.aqa.org.uk/sample-papers-and-mark-schemes/2018/june/AQA-87001-QP-JUN18.PDF, last accessed June 26 2020.
AQA (2018b) *GCSE English Language Paper 2*, https://filestore.aqa.org.uk/sample-papers-and-mark-schemes/2018/june/AQA-87002-QP-JUN18.PDF, last accessed June 26 2020.
AQA (2018c) *GCSE English Literature Paper 2*, https://filestore.aqa.org.uk/sample-papers-and-mark-schemes/2018/june/AQA-87022-QP-JUN18-CR.PDF, last accessed June 26 2020.
Au, W. (2007) 'High-stakes testing and curricular control: A qualitative metasynthesis', *Educational Researcher* 36(5): 258–67.
Ball, S., Kenny, A and Gardiner, D. (1990) 'Literacy politics and the teaching of English', in I. Goodson and P. Medway (eds.) *Bringing English to Order*, Sussex: Falmer Press.
Bartlett, F. (1932) *Remembering: A Study in Experimental and Social Psychology*, Cambridge: Cambridge University Press.
Bayard, P. (trans. J. Mehlman) (2008) *How to Talk About Books You Haven't Read*, London: Granta Publications.
Beach, R. (1993) *A Teacher's Introduction to Reader Response Theories*, Champaign, IL: NCTE.
Benton, M., Teasey, J., Bell, R., and Hurst, K. (1988) *Young Readers Responding to Poems*, London: Routledge.
Benton, P. (1999) 'Unweaving the rainbow: Poetry teaching in the secondary school I', *Oxford Review of Education* 25(4): 521–31.
Benton, P. (2000) 'The Conveyor Belt Curriculum? Poetry teaching in the secondary school II', *Oxford Review of Education* 26(1): 86–93.

References

Benwell, B. (2009) '"A pathetic and racist and awful character": Ethnomethodological approaches to the reception of diasporic fiction', *Language and Literature* 18(3): 300–15.
Bernstein, B. (1964) 'Elaborated and restricted codes: Their social origins and some consequences', *American Anthropologist* 66(6): 55–69.
Billington, J., Dowrick, C., Hamer, A., Robinson, J., and Williams, C. (2010) *An Investigation into the Therapeutic Benefits of Reading in Relation to Depression and Wellbeing*, Liverpool: University of Liverpool and Liverpool Primary Care Trust.
Bleiman, B. (2017) 'Decline and Fall? A-level English: The figures', *Teaching English* 15: 63–64.
Bleiman, B. (2020) *What Matters in English Teaching: Collected Blogs and Other Writings*, London: English and Media Centre.
Board of Education (1921) *The Teaching of English in England* (The Newbolt Report), London: HMSO.
Booth, W. (1983) *The Rhetoric of Fiction*, 2nd edition, Chicago, IL: University of Chicago Press.
Brooks, C. (1947) *The Well Wrought Urn: Studies in the Structure of Poetry*, New York, NY: Reynal and Hitchcock.
Brooks, J., and Brooks, M. (1993) *In Search of Understanding: The Case for Constructivist Classrooms*, Alexandria, VA: ASCD.
Brown, P., and Levinson, S. C. (1987) *Politeness: Some Universals in Language Usage*, Cambridge: Cambridge University Press.
Butler, C. (2018) *Literary Studies Deconstructed: A Polemic*, London: Palgrave.
Cameron, D. (2012) 'Not changing English: Syllabus reform at Oxford', *Changing English* 19(1): 13–22.
Carter, R. (ed.) (1982) *Linguistics and the Teacher*, London: Routledge.
Caviglioni, O. (2019) *Dual Coding With Teachers*, Woodbridge: John Catt.
Clark, C. (2011) *Setting the Baseline: The National Literacy Strategy Trust's First Annual Survey into Reading*, London: National Literacy Trust.
Clark, C., and Rumbold, K. (2006) *Reading for Pleasure: A Research Overview*, London: National Literacy Trust.
Cliff-Hodges, G. (2009) 'Children as readers: What we learn from their conversations about reading', *Education 3-13: International Journal of Primary, Elementary and Early Years Education* 37(2): 165–76.
Cliff-Hodges, G. (2010) 'Reasons for reading: Why literature matters', *Literacy* 44(2): 60–68.
Cremin, T. (2010) 'Motivating children to read through literature', in J. Fletcher, F. Parkhill, and G. Gillon (eds.) *Motivating Literacy Learners in Today's World*, Wellington: New Zealand Council for Educational Research.
Cremin, T., and Myhill, D. (2012) *Writing Voices*, New York: Routledge.
Csikszentmihalyi, M. (1996) *Flow and the Psychology of Discovery and Invention*, New York: Harper Collins.
Csikszentmihalyi, M. (2014) *The Collected Works of Mihaly Csikszentmihalyi, Volume 2: Flow and the Foundations of Positive Psychology*, Dordrecht: Springer.
Culpeper, J. (2001) *Language and Characterization: People in Plays and Other Texts*, London: Pearson.
Cushing, I. (2018) 'Grammar policy and pedagogy from primary to secondary school', *Literacy* 53(3): 170–79.
Cushing, I. (2019) *Text World Theory and the Secondary English Classroom*, Unpublished PhD Thesis, Aston University.
Cushing, I., and Giovanelli, M. (2019) 'Integrating language and literature: A Text World Theory approach', *Journal of Literary Education* 2: 199–222.
Davis, P., Magee, F., Koleva, K., Tangeras, T. M., Hill, E., Baker, H., and Crane, L. (2016) *What Literature Can Do*, https://www.thereader.org.uk/literature-can-investigation-effectiveness-shared-reading-whole-population-health-intervention/, last accessed June 26 2020.
Dawes, L., Fisher, E., and Mercer, N. (1992) 'The quality of talk at the computer', *Language and Learning* 10: 22–25.
Delpit, L. (2006) *Other People's Children: Cultural Conflict in the Classroom*, New York: Norton & Company Inc.
Dennett, D. (1987) *The Intentional Stance*, Cambridge, MA: MIT Press.
DESWO (1989) *English 5-16* (The Cox Report), London: HMSO.

DfE (2013a) *English Language: GCSE Subject Content and Assessment Objectives*, https://assets.publishing.service.gov.uk/government/uploads/system/uploads/attachment_data/file/254497/GCSE_English_language.pdf (last accessed July 10 2020).

DfE (2013b) *English Literature: GCSE Subject Content and Assessment Objectives*, https://assets.publishing.service.gov.uk/government/uploads/system/uploads/attachment_data/file/254498/GCSE_English_literature.pdf (last accessed July 10 2020).

Dickens, C. (1861) *Great Expectations*, London: Chapman and Hall.

Duncan-Andrade, J. (2007) 'Gangstas, Wankstas, and Ridas: Defining, developing, and supporting effective teachers in urban schools', *International Journal of Qualitative Studies in Education* 20(6): 617–38.

Duncan-Andrade, J. (2009) 'Note to educators: Hope required when growing roses in concrete', *Harvard Educational Review* 79(2): 181–94.

Duncan-Andrade, J. (2010a) *What a Coach Can Teach a Teacher: Lessons Urban Schools Can Learn from a Successful Sports Program*, New York: Peter Lang Publishing Inc.

Duncan-Andrade, J. (2010b) 'Note to educators: Hope required when growing roses in concrete', Keynote speech at the *Graduate School of Education: Alumni of Color Conference*, Harvard University, 26 February 2010. http://goo.gl/55BlIm, last accessed August 31 2020.

Duncan-Andrade, J., and Morrell, E. (2008) *The Art of Critical Pedagogy: Lessons Urban Schools Can Learn from a Successful Sports Program*, New York: Peter Lang Publishing Inc.

Dungworth, N., Grimshaw, S., McKnight, C., and Morris, A. (2004) 'Reading for pleasure?: A summary of the findings from a survey of the reading habits of Year 5 pupils', *New Review of Children's Literature and Librarianship* 10: 169–88.

Dymoke, S. (2002) 'The dead hand of the exam: The impact of the NEAB anthology on poetry teaching at GCSE', *Changing English* 9(1): 85–93.

Eaglestone, R. (2018) *Doing English: A Guide for Literature Students*, 4th edition. London: Routledge.

Eaglestone, R. (2019) *Literature: Why It Matters*, Cambridge: Polity Press.

Eco, U. (1979) *The Role of the Reader: Explorations in the Semiotics of Texts*, Bloomington, IN: Indiana University Press.

Edwards, D., and Mercer, N. (2013) *Common Knowledge: The Development of Understanding in the Classroom*, London: Routledge.

Edwards, A. D., and Westgate, D. P. (1994) *Investigating Classroom Talk*, London: Routledge.

Emdin, C. (2016) *For White Folks That Teach in the Hood…And the Rest of Y'All Too: Reality Pedagogy and Urban Education*, Boston: Beacon Press.

Emmott, C., and Alexander, M. (2014) 'Foregrounding, burying and plot construction', in P. Stockwell and S. Whiteley (eds.) *The Cambridge Handbook of Stylistics*, Cambridge: Cambridge University Press, pp. 329–43.

Evans, V., and Green, M. C. (2006) *Cognitive Linguistics: An Introduction*, Edinburgh: Edinburgh University Press.

Fairclough, N. (2014) *Language and Power*, 3rd edn. London: Routledge.

Fish, S. (1980) *Is There a Text in This Class? The Authority of Interpretive Communities*, Cambridge, MA: Harvard University Press.

Fisher, D., Frey, N., and Pumpian, I. (2012) *How to Create a Culture of Achievement in Your School and Classroom*, Alexandria, VA: ASCD.

Flower, L. (1987) 'Interpretive acts: Cognition and the construction of discourse', *Poetics* 16: 109–30.

Forster, E. M. (1927) *Aspects of the Novel*, London: Edward Arnold.

Freire, P. (1970) *Pedagogy of the Oppressed*, UK, USA: Continuum Publishing.

Gavins, J. (2007) *Text World Theory: An Introduction*, Edinburgh: Edinburgh University Press.

Gerrig, R. J. (1993) *Experiencing Narrative Worlds: On the Psychological Activities of Reading*, Haven, CT: Yale University Press.

Gerrig, R. J., and Egidi, G. (2010) '*The Bushwhacked Piano* and the bushwhacked reader: The willing construction of disbelief', *Style* 44(1–2): 189–206.

Gerrig, R., and Rapp, D. (2004) 'Psychological processes underlying literary impact', *Poetics Today* 25(2): 265–81.

Gibbons, A., and Whiteley, S. (2018) *Contemporary Stylistics: Language, Cognition, Interpretation*, Edinburgh: Edinburgh University Press.

Gibbons, S. (2013) 'The aims of English teaching: A view from history', *Changing English* 20(2): 138–47.
Gibbons, S. (2014) *The London Association for the Teaching of English 1947–67: A History*, Trentham.
Gibbons, S. (2017) *English and its Teachers: A History of Pedagogy, Policy and Practice*, London: Routledge.
Gibbs, R. W., Kushner, J. M., and Mills, W. R. (1991) 'Authorial intentions and metaphor comprehension', *Journal of Psycholinguistic Research* 20(1): 11–30.
Giovanelli, M. (2010) 'A text world theory approach to the teaching of poetry', *English in Education* 44(3): 214–31.
Giovanelli, M. (2013) *Text World Theory and Keats' Poetry: The Cognitive Poetics of Desire, Dreams and Nightmares*, London: Bloomsbury.
Giovanelli, M. (2015) 'Becoming an English language teacher: Linguistic knowledge, anxieties and the shifting sense of identity', *Language and Education* 29(5): 416–29.
Giovanelli, M. (2016) 'Text World Theory as cognitive grammatics: A pedagogical application in the secondary classroom', in J. Gavins and E. Lahey (eds) *World-Building: Discourse in the Mind*, London: Bloomsbury Academic, pp. 109–26.
Giovanelli, M. (2017) 'Building fictional worlds: Visual representations, poetry and cognition', *Literacy* 51(1): 26–35.
Giovanelli, M. (2019) 'Experiencing poetry in the literature classroom', in L. Stewart-Shaw and B. Neurhor, (eds) *Experiencing Fictional Worlds*, Amsterdam: John Benjamins, pp. 177–97.
Giovanelli, M., and Mason, J. (2015) '"Well I don't feel that": Schemas, worlds and authentic reading in the classroom', *English in Education* 49(1): 41–55.
Giovanelli, M., and Mason, J. (2016) 'Why you should ditch the canon', *Times Educational Supplement (TES)*, December 2016, pp. 34–35.
Giovanelli, M., and Mason, J. (2018a) *The Language of Literature: An Introduction to Stylistics*, Cambridge: Cambridge University Press.
Giovanelli, M., and Mason, J. (2018b) 'Readers, reading and English', *English in Education* 52(1): 20–24.
Goodwyn, A. (2002) 'Breaking up is hard to do: English teachers and that LOVE of reading', *English Teaching: Practice and Critique* 1(1): 66–78.
Goodwyn, A. (2012) 'The status of literature: English teaching and the condition of literature teaching in schools', *English in Education* 46(3): 212–27.
Goswami, U. (2007) *Cognitive Development: The Learning Brain*, Hove: Psychology Press.
Gove, M. (2012) 'Speech to ASCL', https://www.gov.uk/government/speeches/education-secretary-michael-goves-speech-to-ascl, last accessed 26 June 2020.
Green, M., and Brock, T. C. (2000) 'The role of transportation in the persuasiveness of public narratives', *Journal of Personality and Social Psychology* 79(5): 701–21.
Haber, R. N., and Hershenson, M. (1980) *The Psychology of Visual Perception*, New York: Holt, Rhinehart and Winston.
Hakemulder, F., Kuijpers, M. M., Tan, E. S., Bálint, K., and Doicaru, M. M. (eds.) (2017) *Narrative Absorption*, Amsterdam: John Benjamins.
Hall, G. (2009) 'Texts, readers – and real readers', *Language and Literature* 18(3): 331–37.
Halliday, M. (2002) 'On grammar and grammatics', in J. Webster (ed.) *On Grammar: Vol 1 of the Collected Works of M.A.K. Halliday*, London: Continuum, pp. 384–417.
Harrison, C., and Nuttall, L. (2019) 'Cognitive Grammar and reconstrual: Re-experiencing Margaret Atwood's "The Freeze-Dried Groom"', in L. Stewart-Shaw and B. Neurhor (eds) *Experiencing Fictional Worlds*, Amsterdam: John Benjamins, pp. 135–56.
Hartley, J. (with S. Turvey) (2001) *Reading Groups*, Oxford: Oxford University Press.
Hawkins, P. (2015) *The Girl on the Train*, London: Doubleday.
Heider, F., and Simmel, M. (1944) 'An experimental study of apparent behaviour', *The American Journal of Psychology* 57: 243–59.
Herman, D. (1994) 'Textual 'you' and double deixis in Edna O'Brien's *A Pagan Place*', *Style* 28(3): 378–411.
Herman, D. (2013) *Storytelling and the Sciences of the Mind*, Cambridge, MA: MIT Press.
Hill, S. (2010) *The Small Hand*, London: Profile Books.
Hilliard, C. (2012) *English as a Vocation: The 'Scrutiny' Movement*, Oxford: Oxford University Press.
Hirsch, E. D. (1967) *Validity in Interpretation*, New Haven, CT: Yale University Press.

Hirsch, E. D. (2007) *The Knowledge Deficit: Closing the Shocking Education Gap for American Children*, Boston, MA: Houghton Mifflin Harcourt.

Hirsch, E. D. (2019) *Why Knowledge Matters: Rescuing Our Children From Failed Educational Policies*, Cambridge, MA: Harvard Education Press.

Hirsch Jr, E. D., Kett, J. F., and Trefil, J. S. (1988) *Cultural Literacy: What Every American Needs to Know*, USA: Vintage.

Hogan, P. C. (2004) 'Literature, God and the unbearable solitude of consciousness', *Journal of Consciousness Studies* 11: 116–42.

Holland, N. (1973) *Poems in Persons: An Introduction to the Psychoanalysis of Literature*, New York, NY: Norton.

Hopper, R. (2006) 'The good, the bad and the ugly: Teachers' perception of quality in fiction for adolescent readers', *English in Education* 40(2): 55–70.

Horton, D., and Whohl, R. R. (1956) 'Mass communication and para-social interaction: Observations on intimacy at a distance', *Psychiatry: Interpersonal and Biological Processes* 19(3): 215–29.

Hunt, R. A., and Vipond, D. (1986) 'Evaluations in literary reading', *Text* 6(1): 53–71.

Iser, W. (1974) *The Implied Reader: Patterns of Communication in Prose Fiction from Bunyan to Beckett*, Baltimore, MD: John Hopkins University Press.

Jerrim, J., and Moss, G. (2019) 'The link between fiction and teenagers' reading skills: International evidence from the OECD PISA study', *British Educational Research Journal* 45(1): 181–200.

Johnson, D. (2012) 'Transportation into a story increases empathy, prosocial behavior, and perceptual bias toward fearful expressions', *Personality and Individual Differences* 52(2): 150–55.

Jones, P. E. (2013) 'Bernstein's 'codes' and the linguistics of 'deficit'', *Language and Education* 27(2): 161–179.

Karolides, N. (ed.) (1999) *Reader Response in Secondary and College Classrooms*, 2nd edition, New York, NY: Routledge.

Kidd, D. C., and Castano, E. (2017) 'Different stories: How levels of familiarity with literary and genre fiction relate to mentalizing', *Psychology of Aesthetics, Creativity, and the Arts* 11: 474–86.

King, S. (1978) *The Man Who Loved Flowers* (from the Night Shift collection), USA: Doubleday, pp. 291–96.

King, S. (2012) 'Stephen King on Twilight, 50 Shades of Grey, Lovecraft and more'. University of Massachusetts, Lowell, USA, https://www.youtube.com/watch?v=l8TkQvdJVbc, last accessed 28 August 2020.

Kress, G., Jewitt, C., Bourne, J., Franks, A., Hardcastle, J., Jones, K., and Reid, E. (2005) *English in Urban Classrooms: A Multimodal Perspective on Teaching and Learning*, Abingdon: Routledge.

Lakoff, G. (2004) *Don't Think of an Elephant! Know Your Values and Frame the Debate*, White River Junction, VT: Chelsea Green Publishing Company.

Langacker, R. (2008) *Cognitive Grammar: A Basic Introduction*, New York, NY: Oxford University Press.

Leavis, F. R. (1948) *The Great Tradition*, London: Chatto & Windus.

Lee, K., Talwar, V., McCarthy, A., Ross, I., Evans, A., and Arruda, V. (2014) Can classic moral stories promote honesty in children? *Psychological Science* 25(8): 1630–36.

Leech, G., and Short, M. (2007) *Style in Fiction*, 2nd edition, London: Longman.

Long, R. (2017) 'The problem of subject terminology and the power of 'I like'', https://www.englishandmedia.co.uk/blog/the-problem-with-subject-terminology-and-the-power-of-i-like, last accessed 26 June 2020.

Macken-Horarik, M. (2009) 'Navigational metalanguages for new territory in English; the potential of grammatics, *English Teaching: Practice and Critique* 8(3): 55–69.

Macken-Horarik, M. (2012) 'Why school English needs a 'good enough' grammatics (and not more grammar)', *Changing English: Studies in Culture and Education* 19(2): 179–94.

Mackey, M. (2019) 'Visualization and the Vivid Reading Experience', *Jeunesse: Young People, Texts, Cultures* 11(1): 38–58.

Mar, R. A. (2018) 'Stories and the promotion of social cognition', *Current Directions in Psychological Science* 27(4): 257–62.

Mar, R. A., Oatley, K., Hirsh, J., dela Paz, J., and Peterson, J. B. (2006) 'Bookworms versus nerds: Exposure to fiction versus non-fiction, divergent associations with social ability, and the simulation of fictional social worlds', *Journal of Research in Personality* 40: 694–712.

Marsh, E. J., Butler, A. C., and Umanath, S. (2012) 'Using fictional sources in the classroom: Applications from cognitive psychology', *Educational Psychology Review* 24(3): 449–69.

Mason, J. (2014) 'Narrative', in P. Stockwell and S. Whiteley (eds) *The Cambridge Handbook of Stylistics*, Cambridge: Cambridge University Press, pp. 179–95.

Mason, J. (2016) 'Narrative interrelation, intertextuality and teachers' knowledge of students' reading', in M. Giovanelli and D. Clayton (eds.) *Knowing About Language: Linguistics and the Secondary English Classroom*, London: Routledge, pp. 162–72.

Mason, J. (2019) *Intertextuality in Practice*, Amsterdam: John Benjamins.

Mason, J., and Giovanelli, M. (2017) "What do you think? Let me tell you': Discourse about texts and the literature classroom', *Changing English* 24(3): 318–29.

Maybin, J. (2013) 'What counts as reading? PIRLS, *Eastenders* and *The Man on the Flying Trapeze*', *Literacy* 47(2): 59–66.

McCallum, A. (2012) *Creativity and Learning in Secondary English*, New York, NY: Routledge

McEwan, I. (2001) *Atonement*, London: Jonathan Cape.

Mercer, N. (1995) *The Guided Construction of Knowledge: Talk Amongst Teachers and Learners*, Clevedon: Multilingual Matters.

Miall, D. (2007) *Literary Reading: Empirical and Theoretical Studies*, New York, NY: Perter Lang.

Murphy, S. T., Frank, L. B., Moran, M. B., and Patnoe-Woodley, P. (2011) 'Involved, transported, or emotional? Exploring the determinants of change in knowledge, attitudes, and behavior in entertainment-education', *Journal of Communication* 61(3): 407–31.

Nash, J. (2007) 'The attitudes of English majors to literary study', *Changing English* 14(1): 77–86.

Naylor, A., and Woods, A. (2012) *Teaching Poetry: Reading and Responding to Poetry in the Secondary Classroom*, London: Routledge.

Newton-De Molina, D. (ed.) (1976) *On Literary Intention: Critical Essays*, Edinburgh: Edinburgh University Press.

Nikolajeva, M. (2014). *Reading for Learning: Cognitive Approaches to Children's Literature* (Vol. 3), Amsterdam: John Benjamins Publishing Company.

Nightingale, P. (2011) 'Now you see me, now you don't: From reader to student and back again in A Level English literature', *English in Education* 45(2): 146–60.

Nuttall, L. (2015) 'Attributing minds to vampires in Richard Matheson's *I Am Legend*', *Language and Literature* 24(1): 23–39.

Nuttall, L. (2017) 'Online readers between the camps: A Text World Theory analysis of ethical positioning in *We Need to Talk About Kevin*', *Language and Literature* 26(2): 153–71.

O'Malley, R. (1947) 'English', in D. Thompson and J. Reeve (eds.) *The Quality of Education*, London: Frederick Muller.

Oatley, K. (1994) 'A taxonomy of the emotions of literary response and a theory of identification in fictional narrative', *Poetics* 23(1–2): 53–74.

Oatley, K. (2012) *The Passionate Muse: Exploring Emotion in Stories*, Oxford: Oxford University Press.

OECD (2010) *2009 PISA Technical Report*, Paris: OECD Publishing.

Ofsted (2011) *Moving English Forward: Action to Raise Standards in English*.

Paivio, A. (1971) *Imagery and Verbal Processes*, New York, NY: Holt, Rinehart and Winston.

Paivio, A. (1986) *Mental Representations: A Dual Coding Approach*, New York, NY: Oxford University Press.

Pennac, D. (1992) *Comme un Roman*, Paris: Gallimard.

Peplow, D. (2011) '"Oh, I've known a lot of Irish people": Reading groups and the negotiation of literary interpretation', *Language and Literature* 20(4): 295–315.

Perry, B., and Szalavitz, M. (2007) *The Boy Who Was Raised as a Dog, And Other Stories from a Child Psychiatrist's Notebook*, USA: BasicBooks.

Pomerantz, A. (1984) 'Agreeing and disagreeing with assessments: Some features of preferred-dispreferred turn shapes', in J. M. Atkinson and J. Heritage (eds) *Structures of Social Action: Studies in Conversation Analysis*, Cambridge: Cambridge University Press, pp. 57–101.

Pope, R. (1995) *Textual Intervention: Critical and Creative Strategies for Literary Studies*, Oxon: Routledge.

Potter, J. (1996) *Representing Reality: Discourse, Rhetoric and Social Construction*, London: SAGE.

Priestley, C. (2007) *Uncle Montague's Tales of Terror*, London: Bloomsbury.

Propp, V. (1968) *Morphology of the Folk Tale*, 2nd edition, Austin, TX: University of Texas Press.

Quigley, A. (2020) *Closing the Reading Gap*, London: Routledge.

Richards, I. A. (1929) *Practical Criticism: A Study of Literary Judgement*, London: Routledge.
Riffaterre, M. (1959) 'Criteria for style analysis', *Word* 15: 154–74.
Rosenblatt, L. (1938) *Literature as Exploration*, New York, NY: D. Appleton-Century Company.
Rosenblatt, L. (1978) *The Reader, The Text, The Poem: The Transactional Theory of the Literary Work*, Carbondale and Edwardsville, IL: Southern Illinois University Press.
Rosenblatt, L. (2005) *Making Meaning with Texts: Selected Essays*, Portsmouth.
Rowling, J. K. (1998) *Harry Potter and the Chamber of Secrets*, New York: Scholastic.
Sanford, A. J. (2002) 'Context, attention and depth of processing during interpretation', *Mind and Language* 17(1–2): 188–206.
Sanford, A. J., and Emmott, C. (2012) *Mind, Brain and Narrative*, Cambridge: Cambridge University Press.
Sanford, A. J., and Sturt, P. (2002) 'Depth of processing in language comprehension: Not noticing the evidence', *Trends in Cognitive Sciences* 6(9): 382–86.
Scott, J. (2014) *Creative Writing and Stylistics: Creative and Critical Approaches*, UK: Macmillan International Higher Education.
Snapper, G. (2013) 'Exploring resistance to poetry in Advanced English Studies', in S. Dymoke, A. Lambirth and A. Wilson (eds) *Making Poetry Matter: International Research on Poetry Pedagogy*, London: Bloomsbury, pp. 31–41.
Steele, C. M. (2010) *Whistling Vivaldi: And Other Clues To How Stereotypes Affect Us*, New York: Norton and Company Inc.
Stimpson, C. (1990) 'Reading for love: Canons, paracanons, and whistling Jo March', *New Literary History* 21(4): 957–976.
Stockwell, P. (2002) *Cognitive Poetics: An Introduction*, 1st edition, London: Routledge.
Stockwell, P. (2009) *Texture: A Cognitive Aesthetics of Reading*, Edinburgh: Edinburgh University Press.
Stockwell, P. (2011) 'Authenticity and creativity in reading lamentation', in Joan Swann, Rob Pope and Ronald Carter (eds) *Creativity in Language and Literature: The State of the Art*, Basingstoke: Palgrave Macmillan, pp. 203–16.
Stockwell, P. (2013) 'The positioned reader', *Language and Literature* 22(3): 263–77.
Stockwell, P. (2016) 'The texture of authorial intention', in J. Gavins and E. Lahey (eds) *World Building: Discourse in the Mind*, London: Bloomsbury, pp. 147–64.
Stockwell, P. (2020) *Cognitive Poetics: An Introduction*, 2nd edition, London: Routledge.
Stockwell, P., and Mahlberg, M. (2015) 'Mind-modelling with corpus stylistics in *David Copperfield*', *Language and Literature* 24(2): 129–147.
Sullivan, A., and Brown, M. (2015) 'Reading for pleasure and progress in vocabulary and mathematics', *British Educational Research Journal* 41: 971–91.
The Royal Society of Literature (2017) *Literature in Britain Today*, https://225475-687350-raikfcquaxqncofqfm.stackpathdns.com/wp-content/uploads/2017/02/RSL-Literature-in-Britain-Today_01.03.17.pdf, last accessed 26 June 2020.
Tompkins, J. P. (ed.) (1980) *Reader-Response Criticism: From Formalism to Post-Structuralism*, Baltimore, MD: John Hopkins University Press.
Turner, R. (1968) 'The self-conception in social interaction', in C. Gordon and K. Gergen, *The Self in Social Interaction*, London: John Wiley, pp. 93–107.
Turvey, J., and Lloyd, A. (2014) '*Great Expectations* and the complexities of teacher development', *English in Education* 48(1): 76–92.
Ungerer, F., and Schmid, H. J. (2013) *An Introduction to Cognitive Linguistics*, New York: Routledge.
Vezzali, L. Stathi, S., Giovannini, D., Capozza, D., and Trifiletti, E. (2015) 'The greatest magic of *Harry Potter*: Reducing prejudice', *Journal of Applied Psychology* 45(2): 105–121.
Vipond, D., and Hunt, R. A. (1984) 'Point-driven understanding: Pragmatic and cognitive dimensions of literary reading', *Poetics* 13: 261–77.
Walton, K. L. (1990) *Mimesis as Make-Believe: On the Foundations of the Representational Arts*, Cambridge, MA: Harvard University Press.
Weaven, M., and Clark, T. (2013) '"I guess it scares us"—Teachers discuss the teaching of poetry in senior secondary English', *English in Education* 47(3): 197–212.
Webb, J. (2019) *How to Teach English Literature: Overcoming Cultural Poverty*, Woodbridge: John Catt.

Welleck, R., and Warren, A. (1949) *Theory of Literature*, New York, NY: Harcourt, Brace & Co.

Werth, P. (1999) *Text Worlds: Representing Conceptual Space in Discourse*, London: Longman.

Whiteley, S. (2011a) 'Text World Theory, real readers and emotional responses to *The Remains of the Day*', *Language and Literature* 20(1): 23–41.

Whiteley, S. (2011b) 'Talking about "An Accommodation": The implications of discussion group data for community engagement and pedagogy', *Language and Literature* 20(3): 236–56.

Whiteley, S., and Canning, P. (2017) 'Reader response research in stylistics', *Language and Literature* 26(2): 71–87.

Wimsatt, W. K., and Beardsley, M. C. (1946) 'The intentional fallacy', *Sewanee Review* 54: 468–88.

Wimsatt, W. K., and Beardsley, M. C. (1949) 'The affective fallacy', *Sewanee Review* 57(1): 31–55.

Wolf, M., and Barzillai, M. (2009) 'The importance of deep reading', *Educational Leadership* 66(6): 32–37.

Xerri, D. (2013) 'Colluding in the 'torture' of poetry: Shared beliefs and assessment', *English in Education* 47(2): 134–46.

APPENDIX

Talking About Texts survey

Talking About Texts: Reading and Identity

This questionnaire will ask you questions about your feelings about reading and your experiences of talking about books with other people. It is part of a research project looking at how we think about our reading habits in relation to our identity. By 'reading' we mean physical books, e-books and audio books: we don't mind how you've 'read' them! The questionnaire is completely anonymous – not even the researcher will be able to find out who you are: you won't be asked for your name, your email or any information that could link the answers you give back to you, and the questionnaire won't save this information. There will be one question about which profession you work in, but this is just so we can see if people in particular jobs might think differently about what they read and like (or dislike) in relation to who they are. This does mean that once you submit your answers, you're unlikely to be able to withdraw from the study as we won't be able to link your responses back to you to know which ones to delete. There's no obligation for you to take part and if you change your mind at any point just close the questionnaire before you submit. Your responses will be used in academic research: this means that the anonymous responses might appear in conference papers and publications. The questionnaire should take around 15 minutes to complete. Thank you for your participation. This study was approved by UREC with Converis number ER15871224. Further information at https://www.shu.ac.uk/research/ethics-integrity-and-practice

1. I have read the Participant Information about this study and I am happy the research has been explained to me.
   ○ Yes
   ○ No

2. I understand that I am free to withdraw from the study by closing the questionnaire before submitting my responses, without giving a reason for my withdrawal and without any consequences to my future treatment by the researcher.
   ○ Yes
   ○ No

3. I agree to answer the questionnaire under the conditions of confidentiality set out in the Information above.
    ○ Yes
    ○ No

4. I wish to participate in the study under the conditions set out in the Participant Information above.
    ○ Yes
    ○ No

5. I consent to the information collected for the purposes of this research study, anonymised as explained in the information above (so that I cannot be identified), to be used for any other research purposes.
    ○ Yes
    ○ No

Section 1 of 10

6. What's your favourite book? (You can list up to three if you can't decide).

Section 2 of 10

7. Would you call yourself 'a reader'?
    ○ Yes
    ○ No
    ○ It depends

8. Can you explain your last answer?

Section 3 of 10

9. Have you ever read and enjoyed a book that you'd be reluctant to tell others about?
    ○ Yes
    ○ No
    ○ Can't remember

10. If yes, can you think of any specific examples?

11. If yes, can you elaborate on why you felt this way?

Section 4 of 10

12. Are there any circumstances in which you might lie about reading a book you hadn't read?

13. If so, if you can think of any, please list any books you may have told someone that you'd read when in fact you hadn't.

Section 5 of 10

14. Have you ever felt judged for liking or disliking a particular book, author or genre?

15. If so, can you think of any examples of a time when you felt this way?

Section 6 of 10

16. Do you think a person's taste in books, films or television shows tells you anything about them?

Section 7 of 10

17. Do you ever feel embarrassed about books you haven't read?
    - Yes
    - No

18. Could you say a bit more about this?

Section 8 of 10

19. Roughly, how many books do you read in an average year? (You can include audio books and books you've read on an e-reader.)
    - None
    - 1 to 5
    - 6 to 10
    - 11 to 15

○ 16 to 20
○ 21 to 25
○ More than 25

Section 9 of 10

20. Reflecting on your answers, are there any responses where you haven't been entirely honest, or felt a temptation to lie?
    ○ Yes
    ○ No

21. If you're willing to elaborate, please do so below:

Section 10 of 10

22. How would you best describe your job or profession? (This can be a current or previous role.)

    Anything more to add?

23. Any other thoughts or comments you'd like to share?

INDEX

attention 2, 4, 8, 41, 48–61, 65, 68–70, 72–73, 85; attentional attractors 50–51, 54
authentic reading 6–11, 36, 42, 57
authors 4–5, 43, 45, 59, 66, 87, 90–93, 95, 96, 107, 110; authorial intention 4, 86; real/implied authors 83–84, 87, 90–93; *see also* mind-modelling

Bayard, Pierre 9, 22
Benton, Michael 101
booktalk 22, 24, 26–27, 34
Booth, Wayne 83–86
Bronte, Charlotte 37, 91
burying 48, 52–53, 56–57, 61–63
Butler Act 15–16
Butler, Catherine 97–98

Cambridge English 15–16
canonical texts 4, 16, 18–19, 34, 42–44, 46–47, 91, 99, 107
Carter, Ron 2, 5
characters 66, 84, 86, 94, 98, 100, 102–107; character study 104; flat and round 102; modelling characters 101
characterisation 16, 64, 97, 101–102, 104
children's literature 4, 36, 44, 47
classics 4, 18–19, 31–34, 44
classroom discourse 77–78, 92
cognitive grammatics 3, 75
cognitive linguistics 1–3, 39, 50, 57, 69, 71, 82, 84, 110
cognitive poetics 1, 3, 5, 20, 26, 39, 50, 63, 81–82, 110
cognitive psychology 4, 49, 57, 69
Coleridge, Samuel 77, 78, 91
core knowledge (Hirsch) 17–18
Cox models, the 13
Culpeper, Jonathan 102

cultural capital 17, 19, 32, 43–44
cultural literacy (Hirsch) 18, 42, 44
curriculum 9, 11–14, 16–18, 24, 32–37, 42–46, 83, 90–91, 107, 110

Dickens, Charles 2, 78, 83–84, 91, 103, 109; *Great Expectations* 83, 103–104; *Dombey and Son* 2
disbelief 78–79
discourse-world 69–70, 95
double-deixis 106
Duncan-Andrade, Jeffrey 18, 43, 45, 47

efferent stance 68–69
empathy 3, 107–109
enactors 105–107
English classroom 4, 7, 20, 23–24, 56
English education 3, 15–19, 23, 30, 36, 69
English teacher 26, 30–31
equity 16–17, 44
extra-textual knowledge 76–77, 89

Fish, Stanley 65, 67, 68
figure-ground 48–51, 53–54, 56, 58, 62–63, 72, 90
foreshadowing 61–62
Freire, Paulo 17–19
function-advancing propositions 71, 74, 76

GCSE 37, 77, 93–94, 99, 103–104, 106
Gerrig, Richard 36, 57–59, 63, 78–79
Giovanelli, Marcello 5, 19, 26, 42–43, 63, 75, 77–80, 96, 105, 109
Goodreads 57, 89
Goodwyn, Andrew 10, 36
Grammar school 15–16, 34
grammatics 2–3, 5, 75
group talk 77, 98

Halliday, Michael 2, 5, 75
Harry Potter 36, 51, 109
Herman, David 4, 84–86, 96, 106
Higher Education 11, 14, 17, 21–22, 25, 38, 42
Hill, Susan 70, 72
Hirsch, E. D. 17–19, 44, 82–83, 96

identification 108
immersion 48, 57–58, 60, 63, 78
intentionality 4, 81–90, 92, 95–96
interpretation 8–9, 12, 40, 44–45, 51, 67–68, 75–76, 82–83, 98; feelings 100–101; interpretive communities 65; *see also* manufactured readings

Keats, John 76–77, 88–89, 91; 'The Living Hand' 76–77, 88–89
King, Stephen 7–8, 36, 53, 55, 57, 90; 'The Man Who Loved Flowers' 53–57, 61
knowledge-filling 77, 101

literary reading 2, 67, 75, 78, 81, 85–87, 95, 107
literary transaction 95
literature curriculum 9, 18, 45–46
Local Education Authorities (LEA) 15
London Association for the Teaching of English (LATE) 15
London English 15–16

manufactured readings 8–10, 19, 44, 69, 77
Mason, Jessica 3, 5, 8, 19, 25, 28, 39, 42–43, 63, 75, 77, 79, 80, 96
McEwan, Ian 85–86
metonymy 90
mind-modelling 81, 87, 89, 94, 96, 102, 104, 109
modality 56, 69, 72–73, 76, 78

narrative schema 40–42, 61; *see also* schema theory
narrative world salience 52
narrator 85
national curriculum 13, 90–91
negation 55, 72–73, 78
New Criticism 66, 81, 94

Oatley, Keith 100, 109

paracanon 46
pedagogy 2, 5, 17, 19, 35, 93, 101, 107; critical pedagogy 17
poetry 14, 65, 75, 77, 79, 86, 88, 90, 98, 99, 106, 109

pre-figuring 4, 41, 48, 62–63, 101
professional identity 26, 30–31

questionnaire 4, 20, 26–27, 29, 120–123

reader-response 7, 64–66, 68, 75, 79, 81, 87
reading: first time reading 20, 22, 40–41, 53–54, 61; re-reading 19, 20, 22, 34, 40–41, 104
reading experience 4, 7–9, 21, 23, 25, 57, 67, 69, 75, 94, 96, 102, 105, 107–108, 110; reading for pleasure 7, 9, 11, 23, 57–58, 98; recreational reading 67; *see also* authentic reading
Rosenblatt, Louise 7, 66–68, 79, 95

salience 52, 54, 56
schema 2, 38–42, 61, 65, 90, 100
schema theory 38–40; decay 42; accretion 39, 41, 100; reinforcement 39
schematic knowledge 10, 39–40, 42, 74–75, 102
self-conception 25–26
Shakespeare, William 1, 12, 36, 37, 39, 43, 77, 84, 89–91, 95
Shelley, Mary 51, 105
social action 108–109
social justice 18, 97, 99, 107, 109–110
social media 26, 30, 37
split discourse-world 70, 95
Stockwell, Peter 4, 5, 39–40, 50, 52, 58, 63, 79, 84, 87–88, 96, 102, 109
stylistics 1, 3, 20, 26, 47, 56

Talking About Texts: Reading and Identity 4, 20, 26–30
teacher-led approaches 18, 38, 75
text choices 3, 35–47, 64, 110
Text World Theory 4, 64, 67–71, 74–78, 80, 81, 83, 100, 102, 105, 109; text-world diagrams 71
Theory of Mind 87
Times Educational Supplement (TES) 42–43; *see also* mind-modelling
toggling 48
transactional theory 4, 64, 67, 69, 70, 81–82, 87, 101
transportation 48, 57–60, 63, 78

Walton, Kendall 100
world-building 70, 72, 75–76
writers 81–96; models of the writer 83, 89; *see also* author

Young Adult fiction 42–43

Taylor & Francis eBooks

www.taylorfrancis.com

A single destination for eBooks from Taylor & Francis with increased functionality and an improved user experience to meet the needs of our customers.

90,000+ eBooks of award-winning academic content in Humanities, Social Science, Science, Technology, Engineering, and Medical written by a global network of editors and authors.

TAYLOR & FRANCIS EBOOKS OFFERS:

- A streamlined experience for our library customers
- A single point of discovery for all of our eBook content
- Improved search and discovery of content at both book and chapter level

REQUEST A FREE TRIAL
support@taylorfrancis.com

Printed in Great Britain
by Amazon